# this book belongs to

· · · · · · · · · · · · · · · · · · · · · · · · · · · · · · ·

# COLOR TEST PAGE

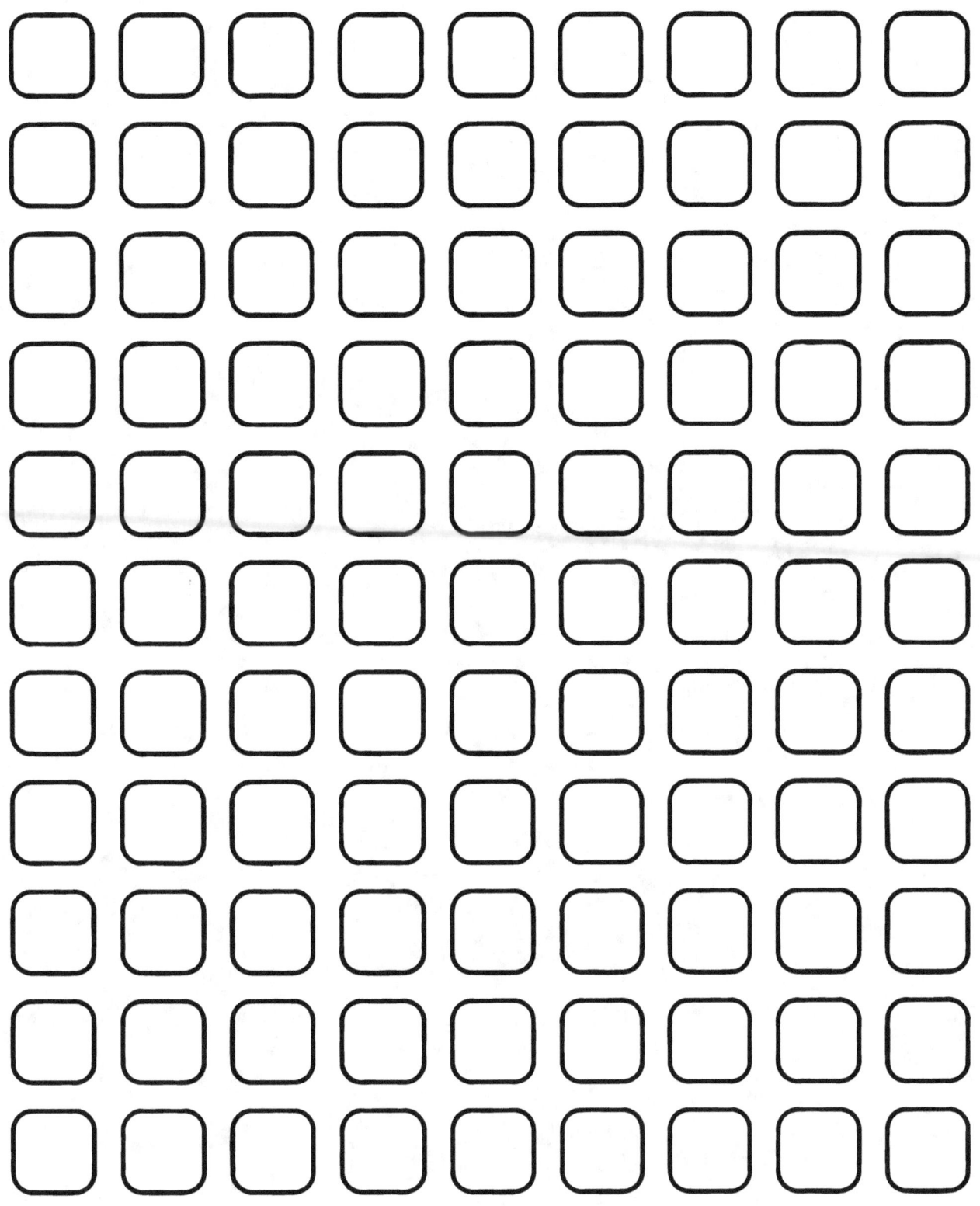

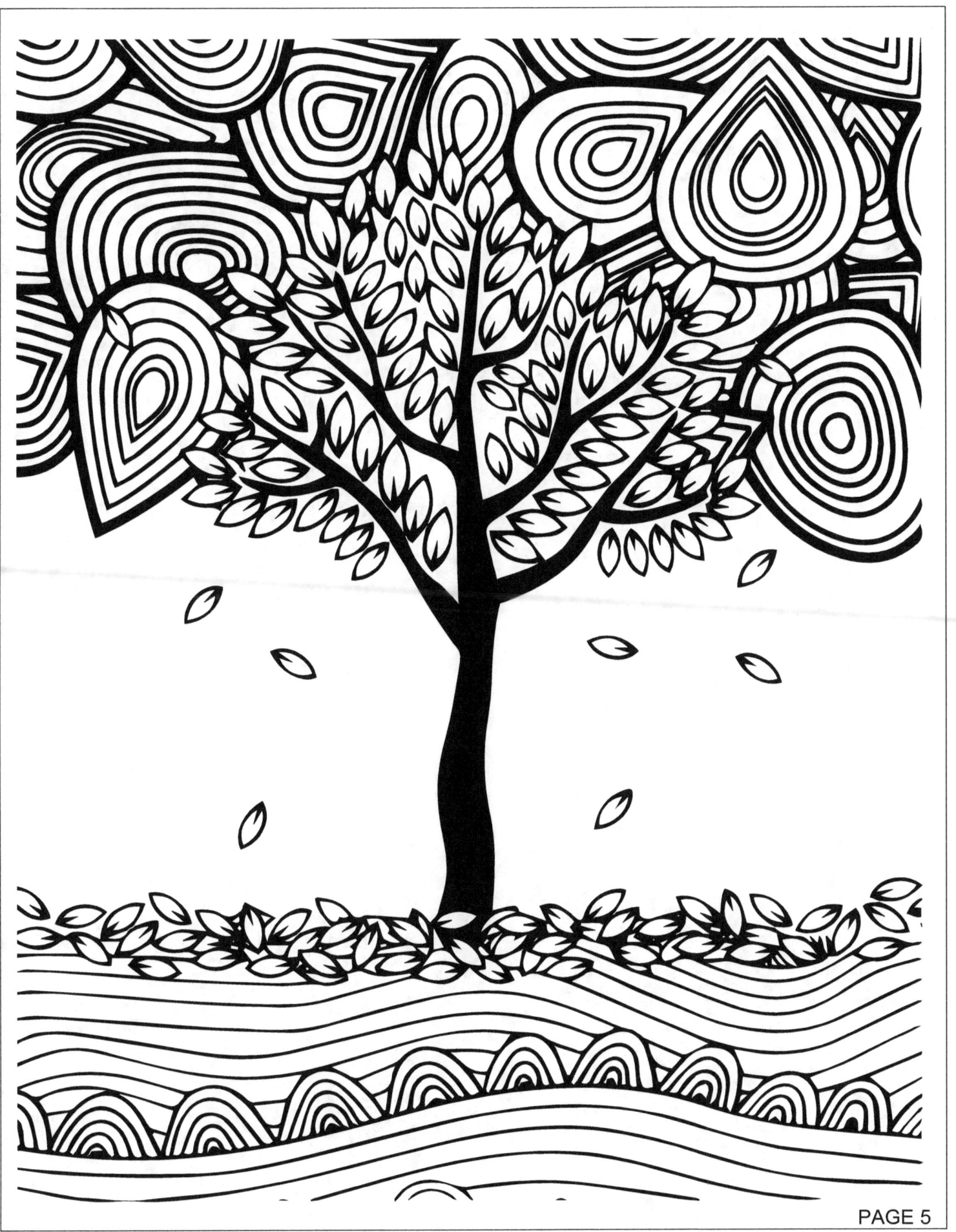

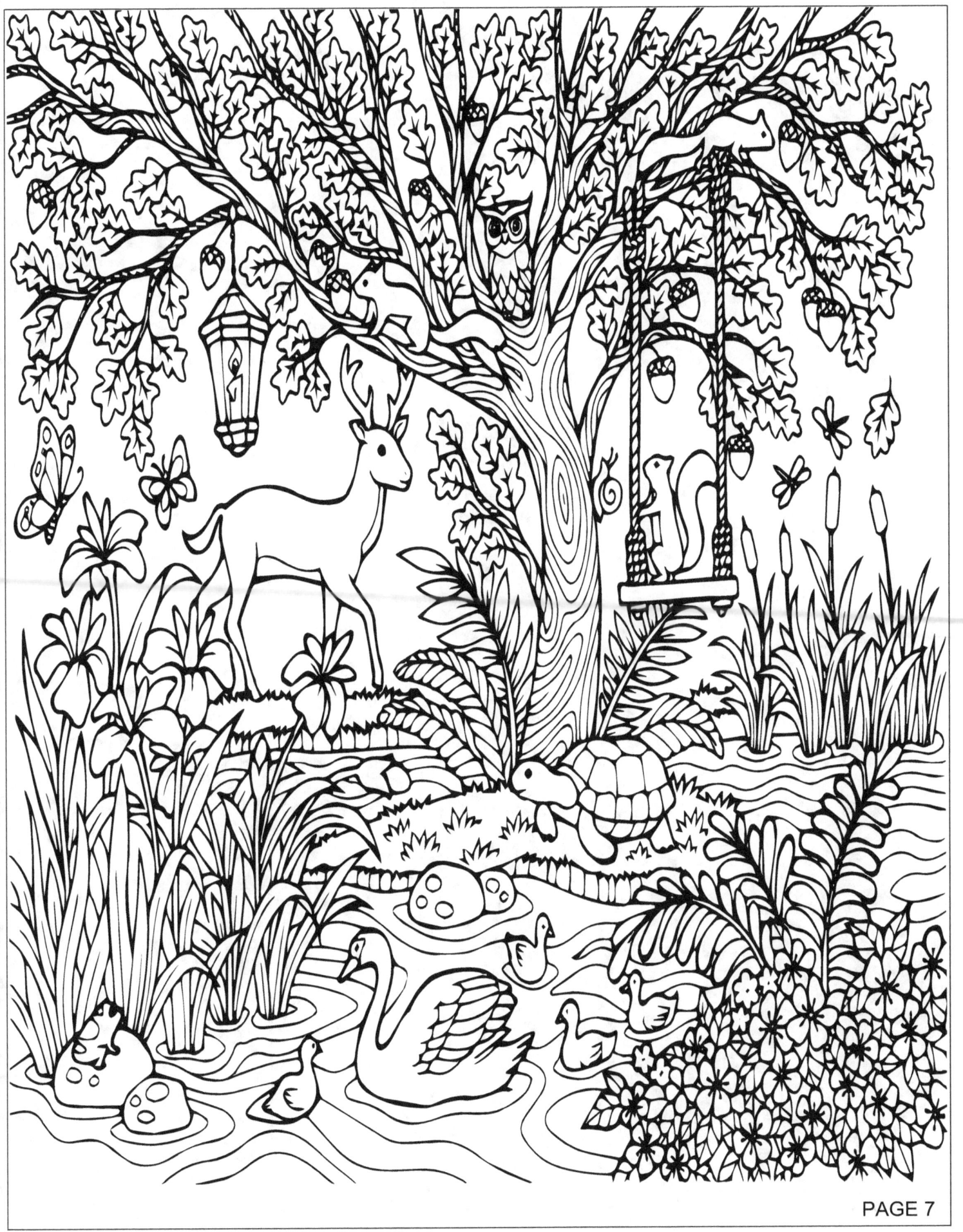

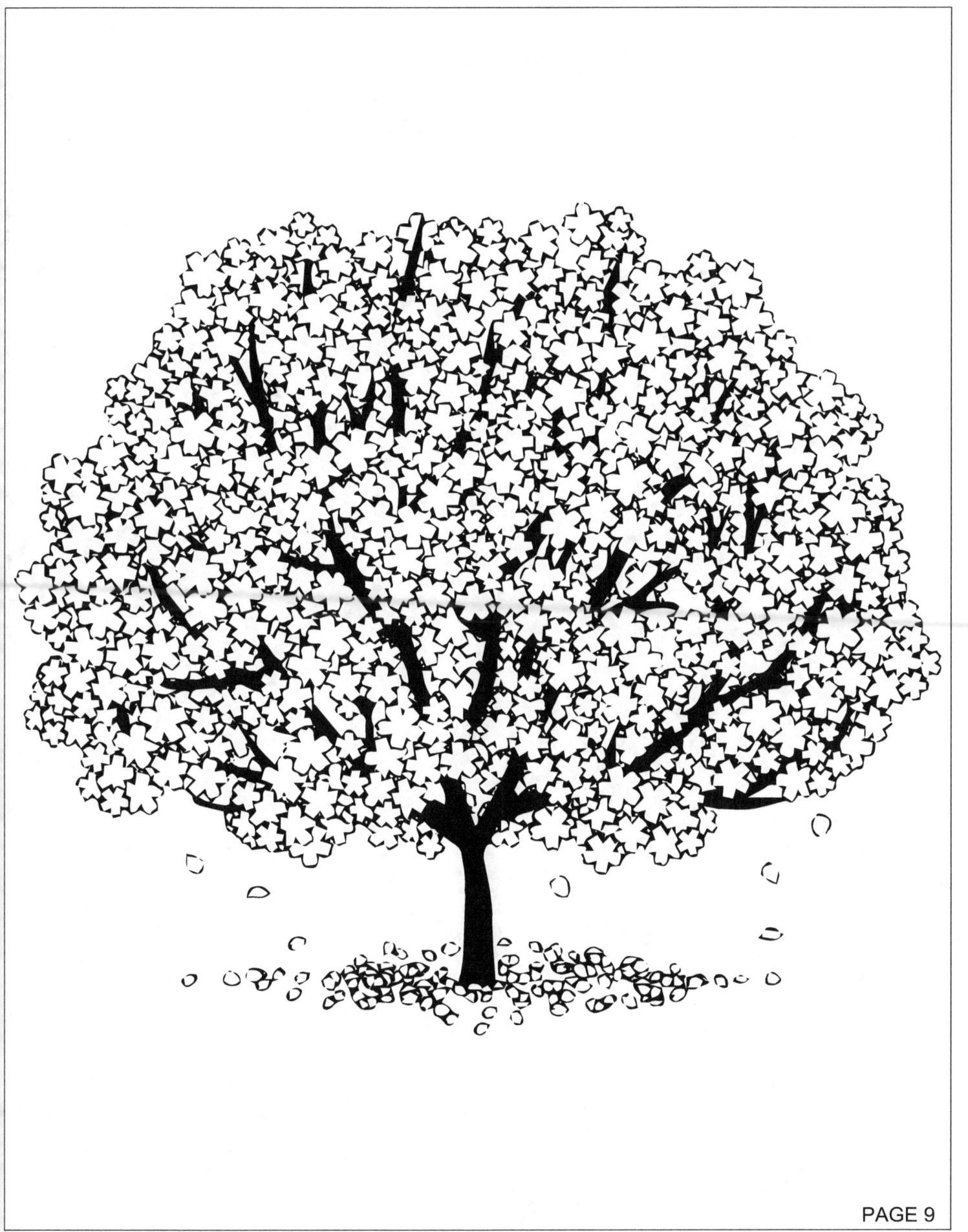

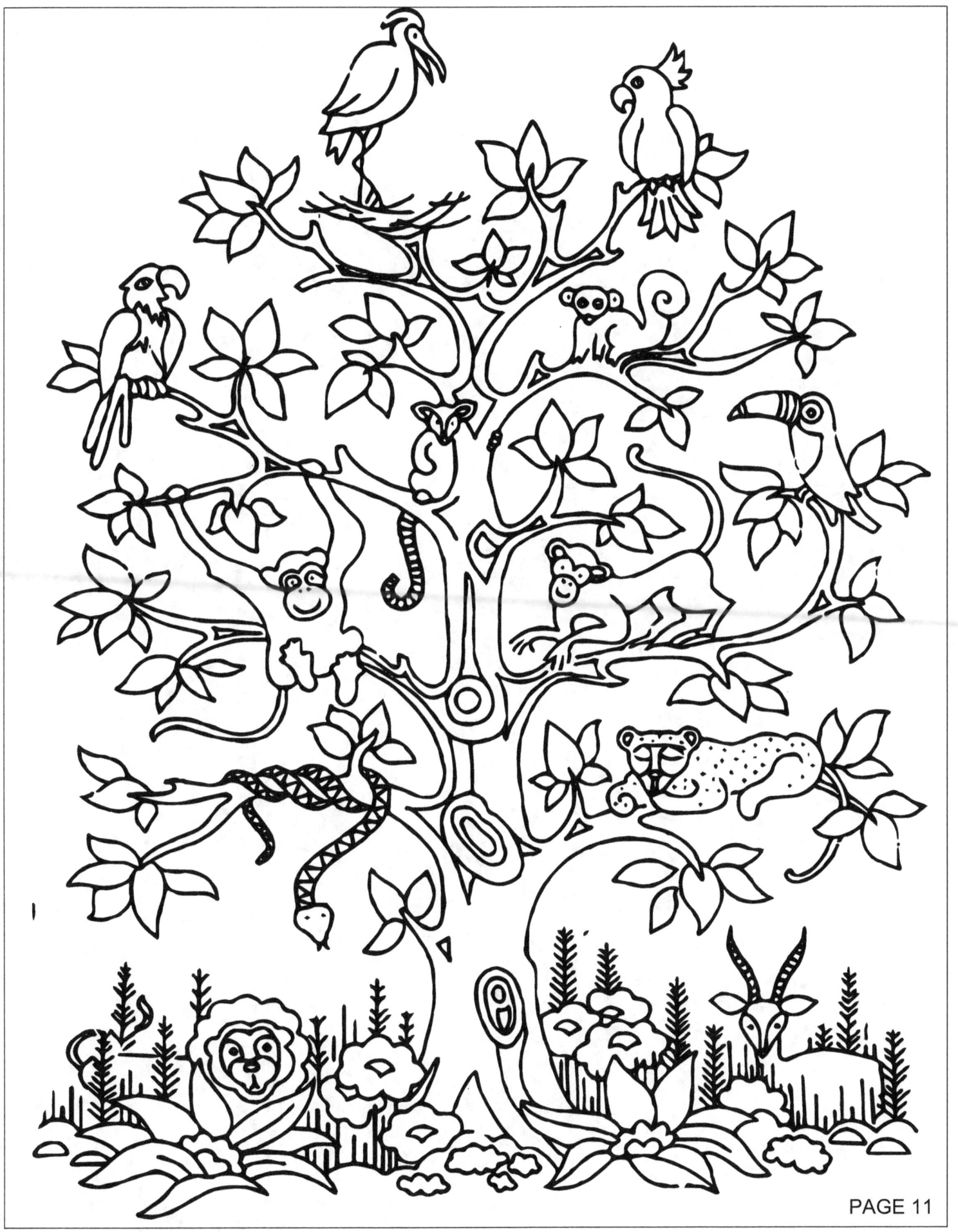

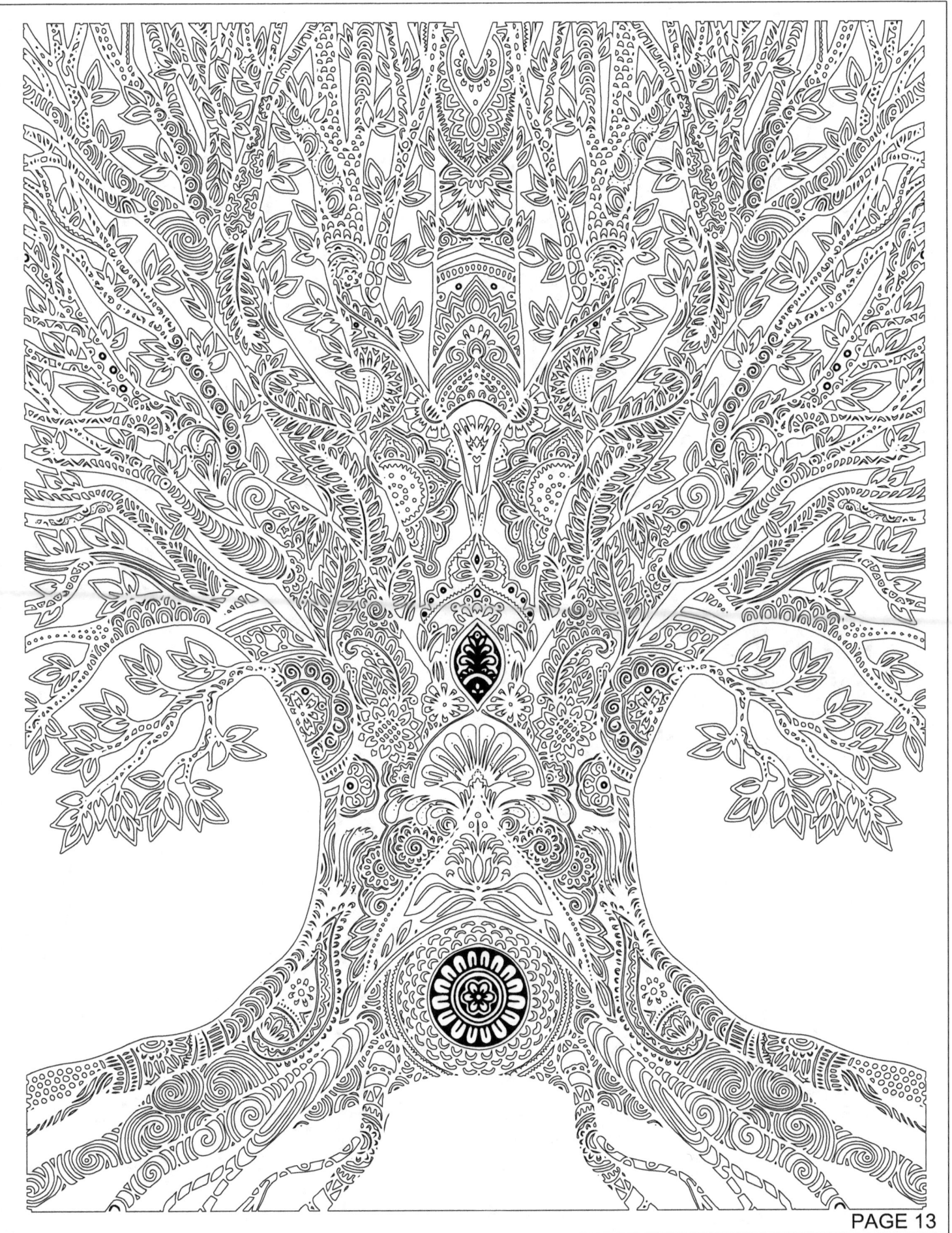

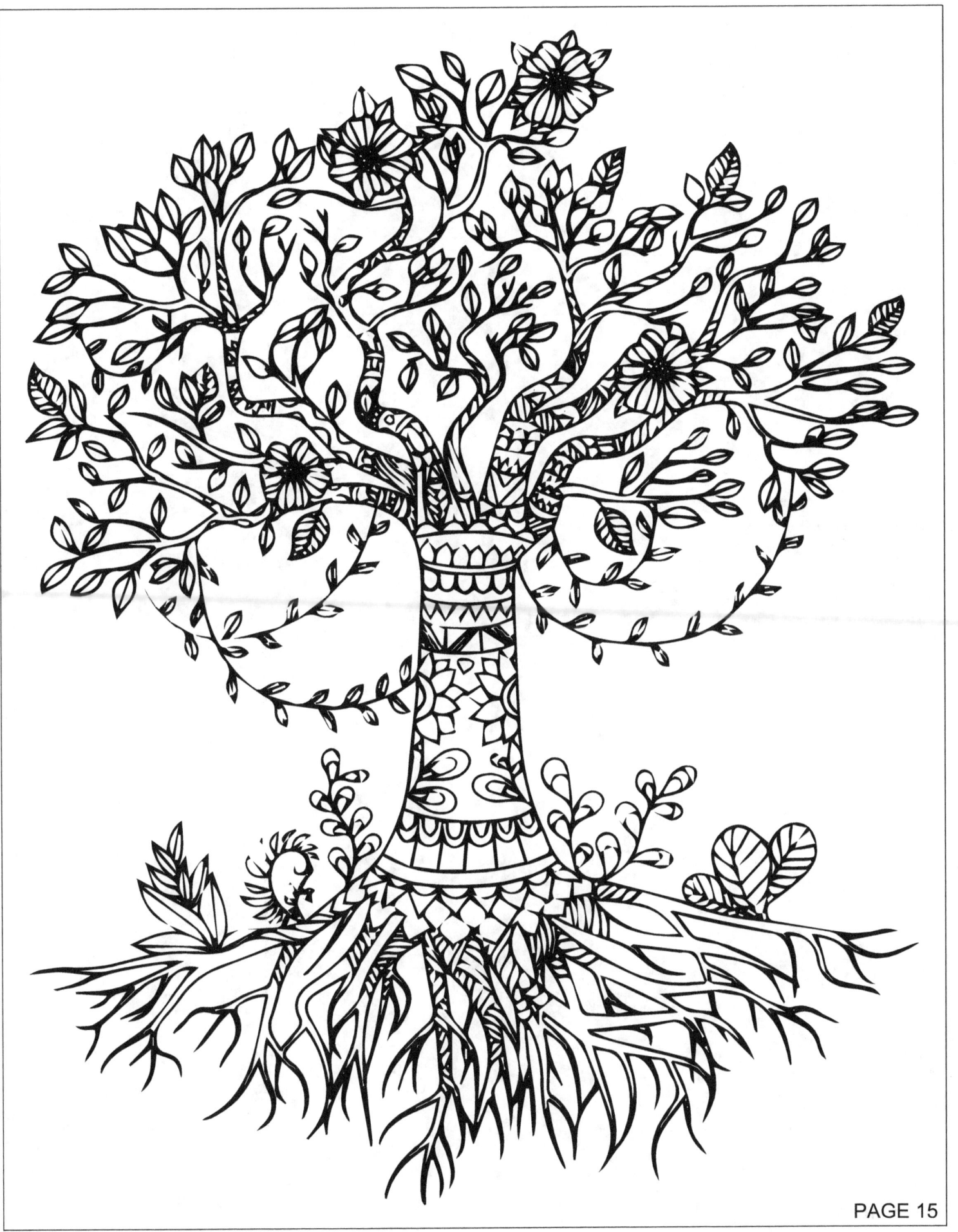

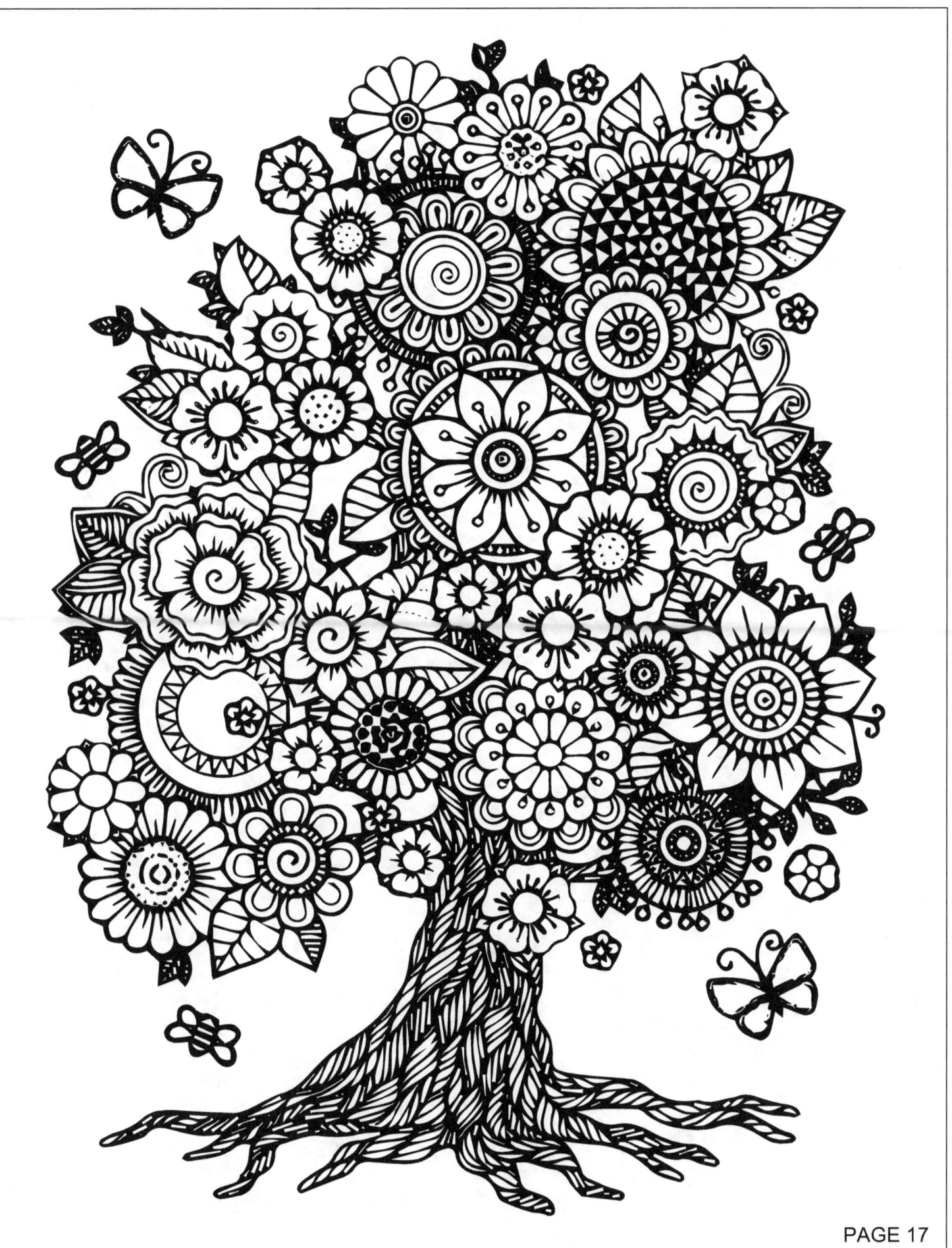

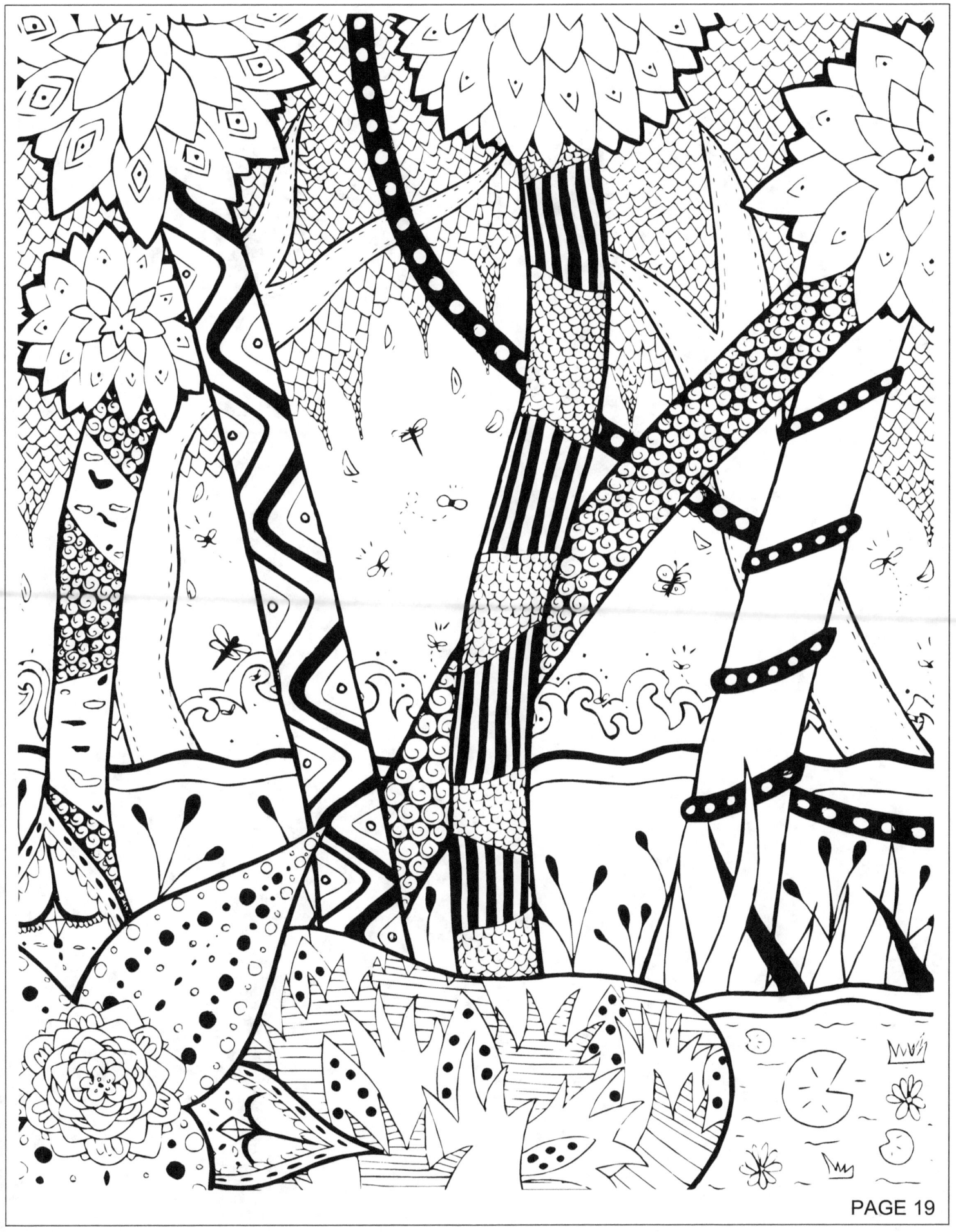

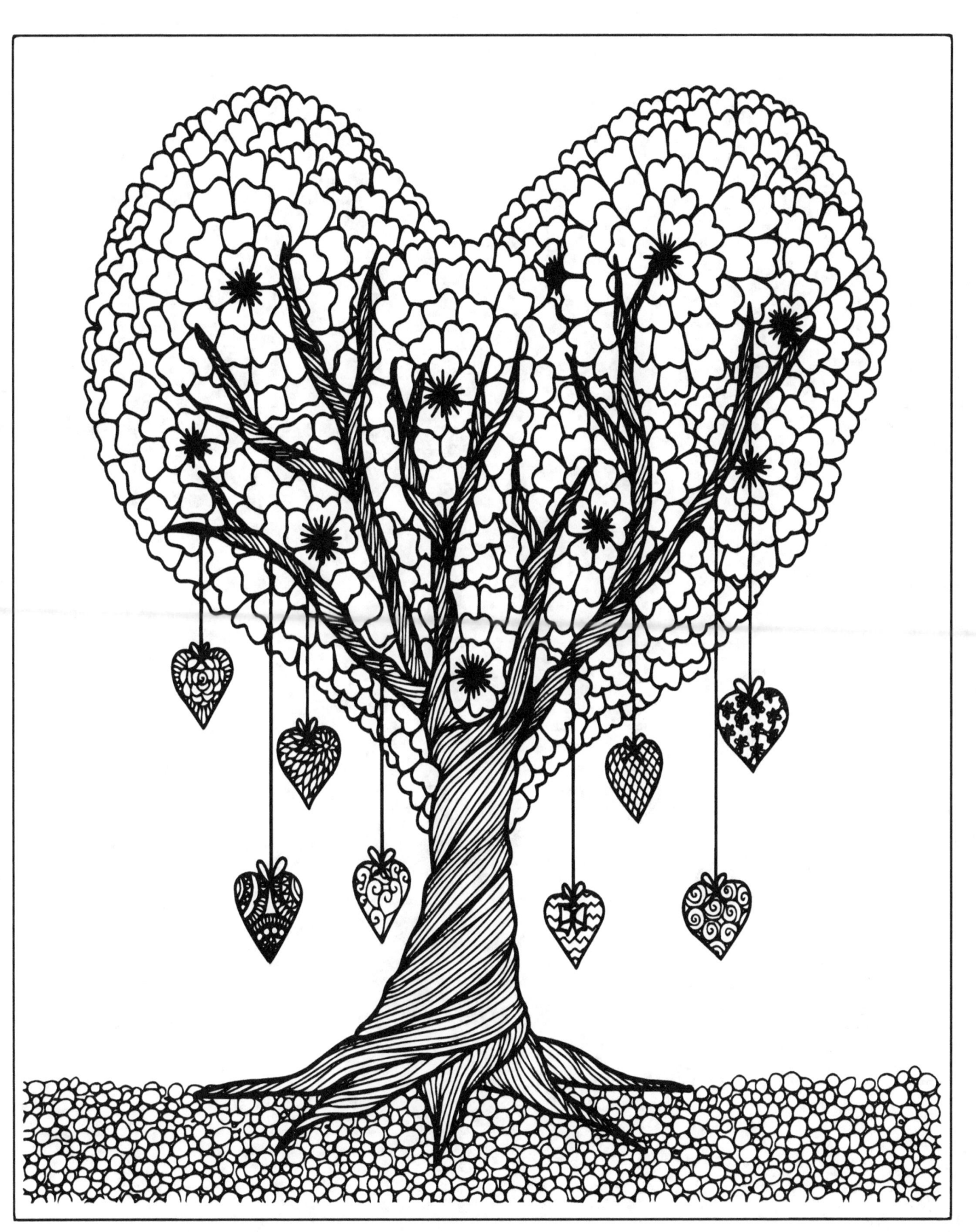

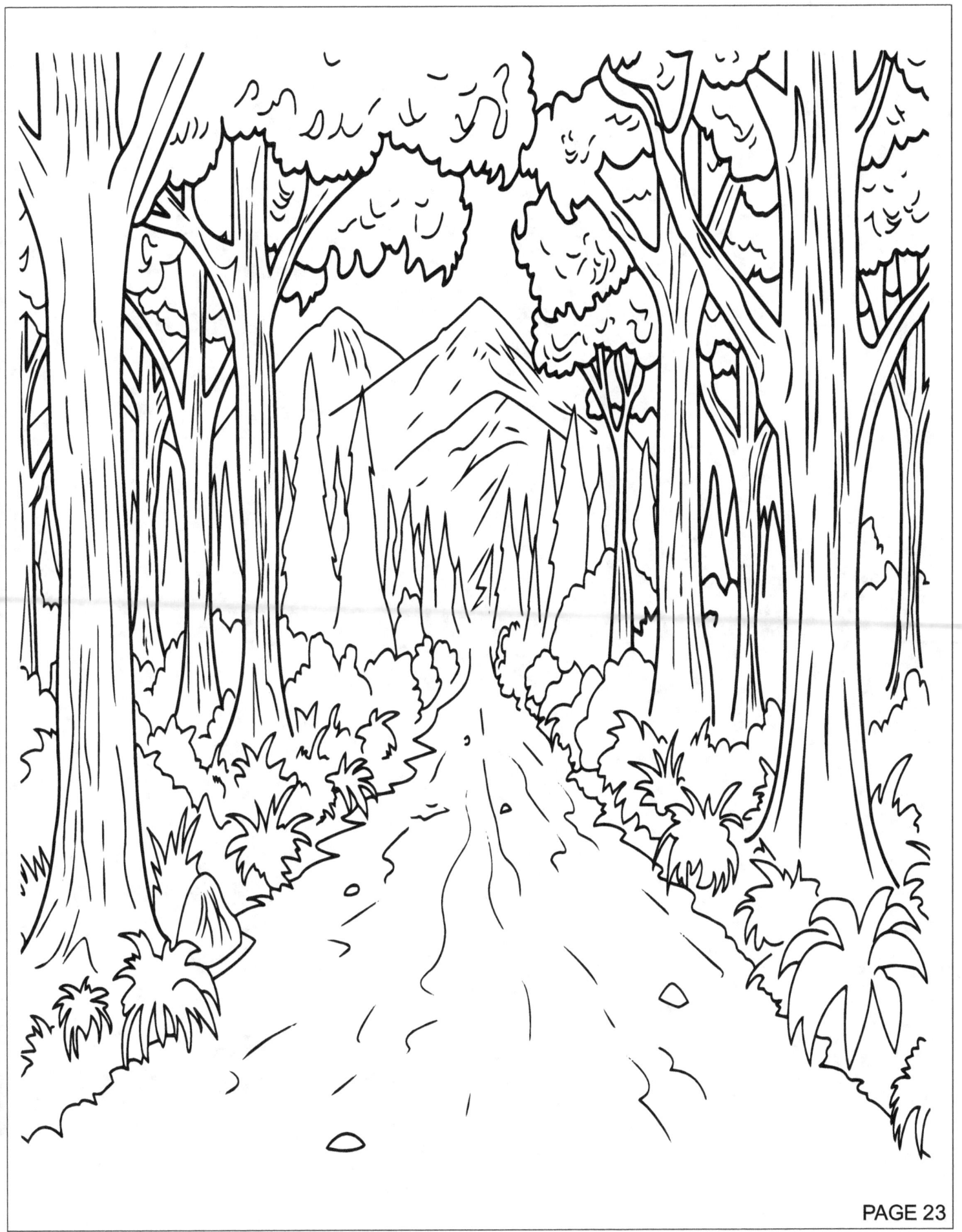

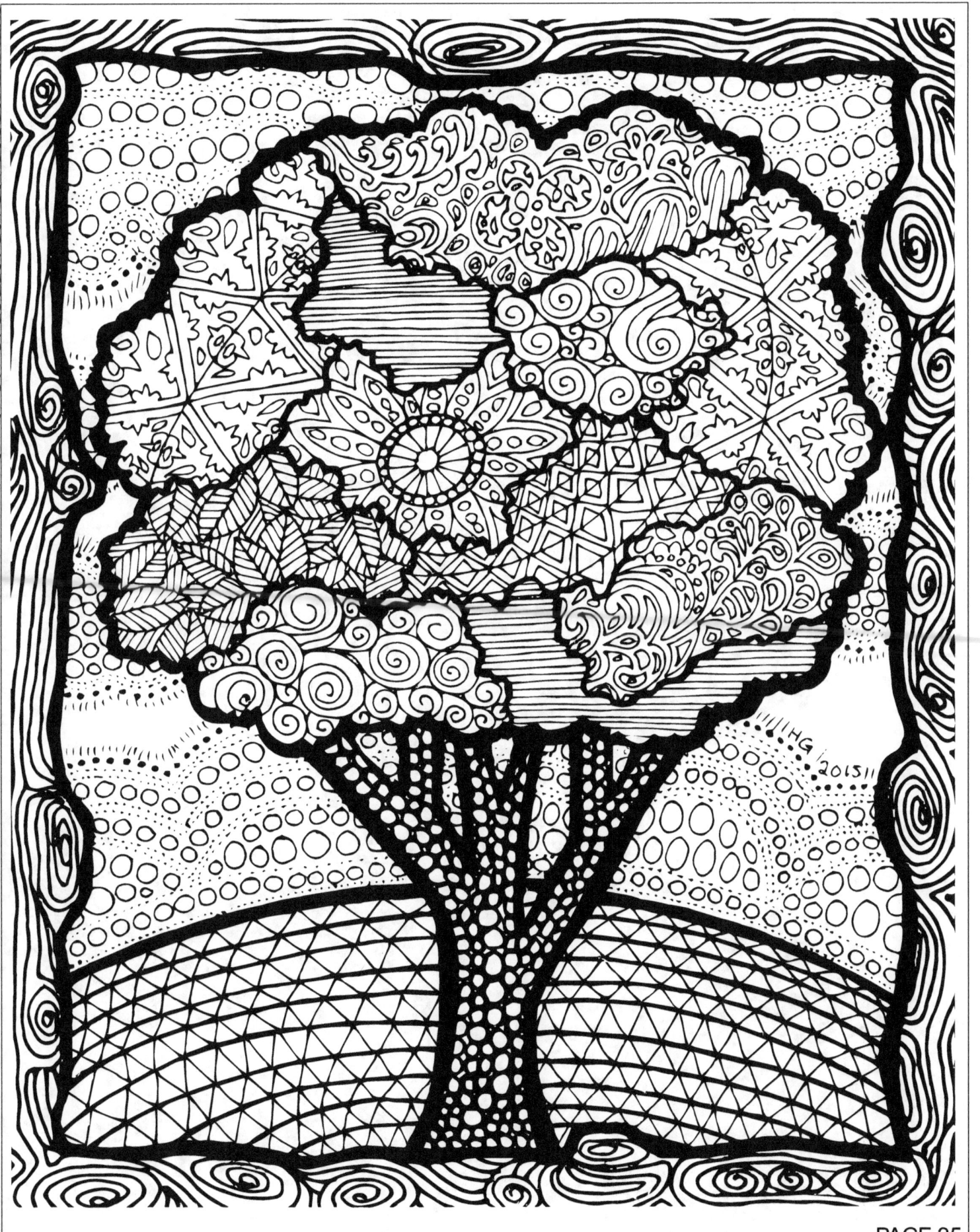

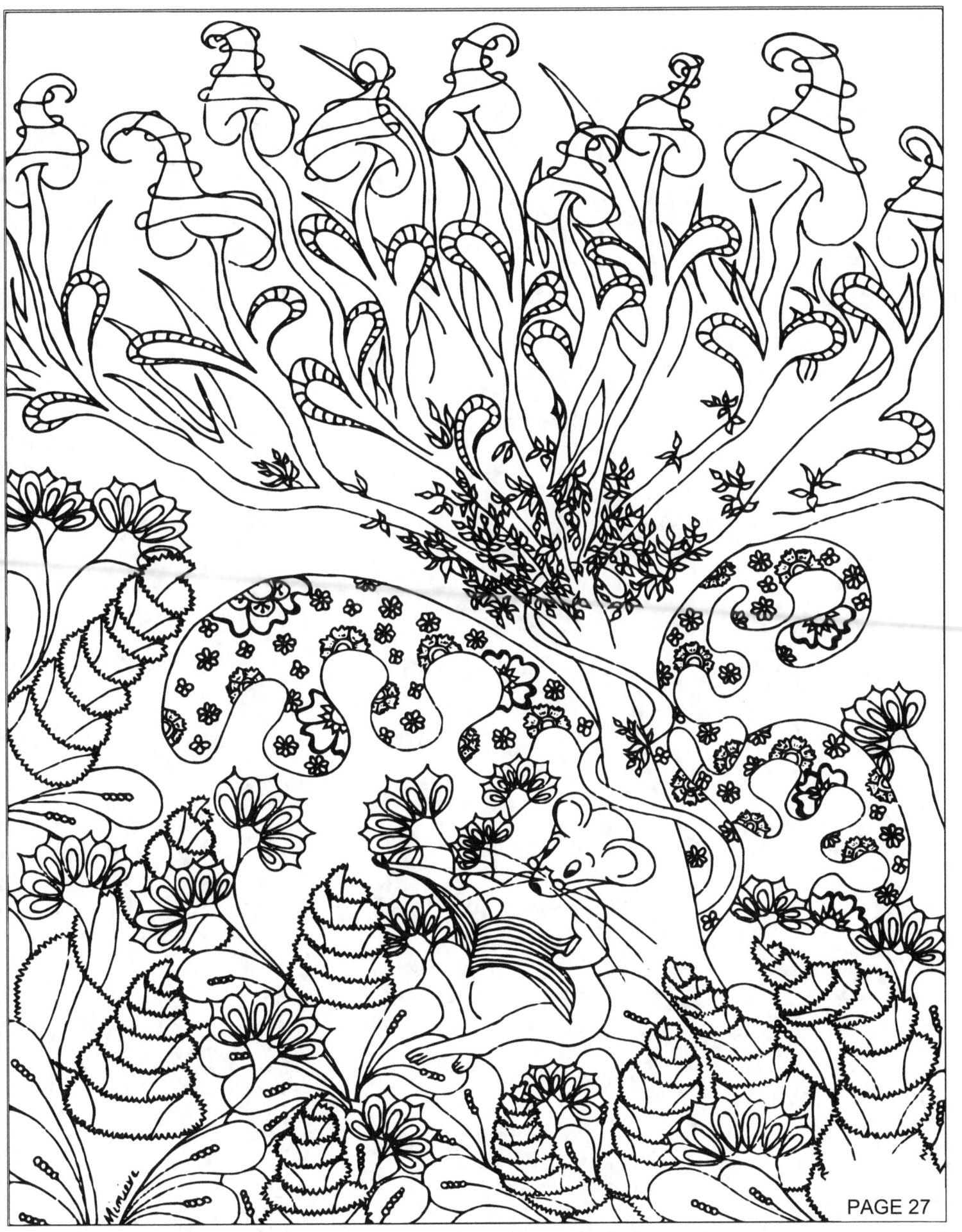

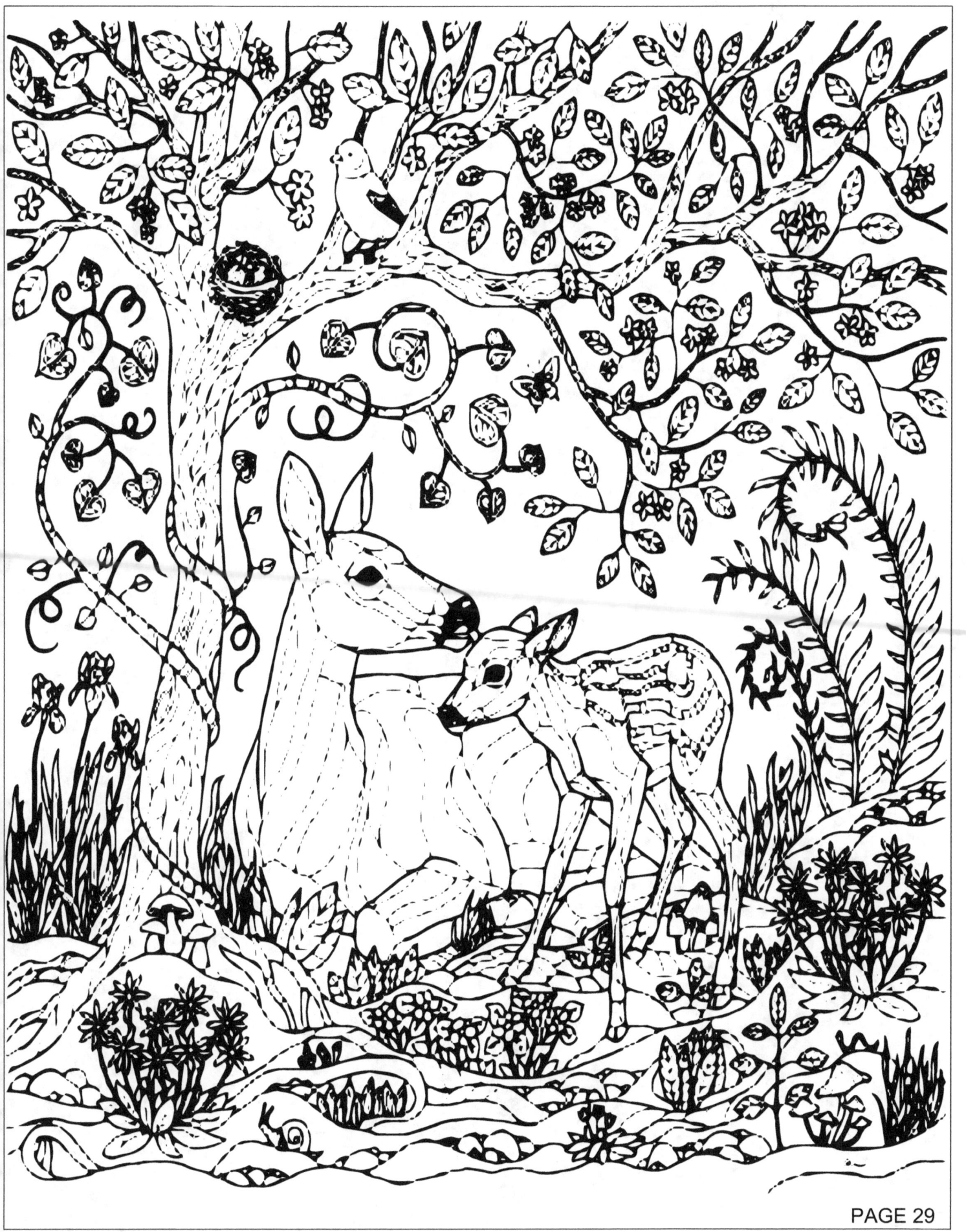

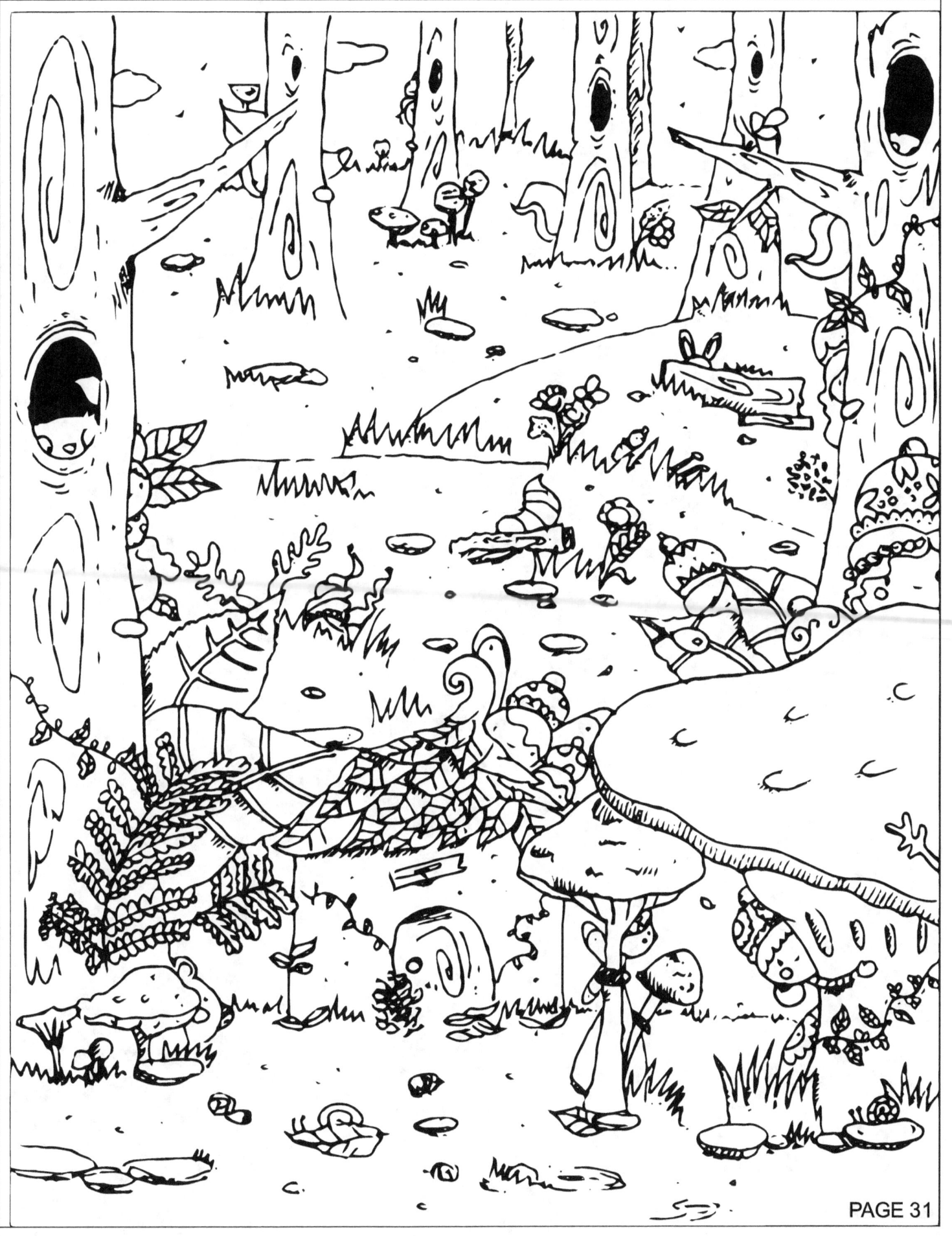

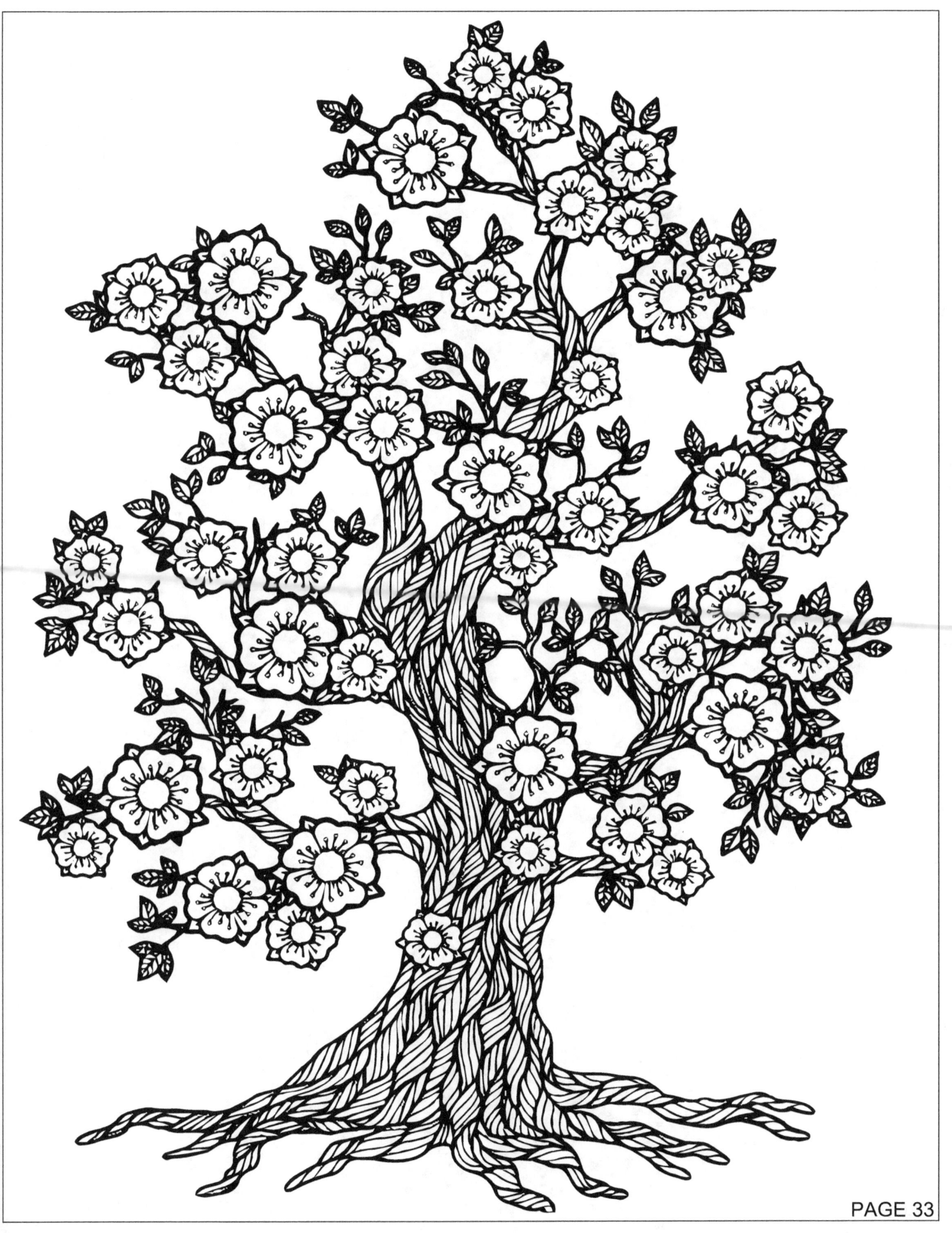

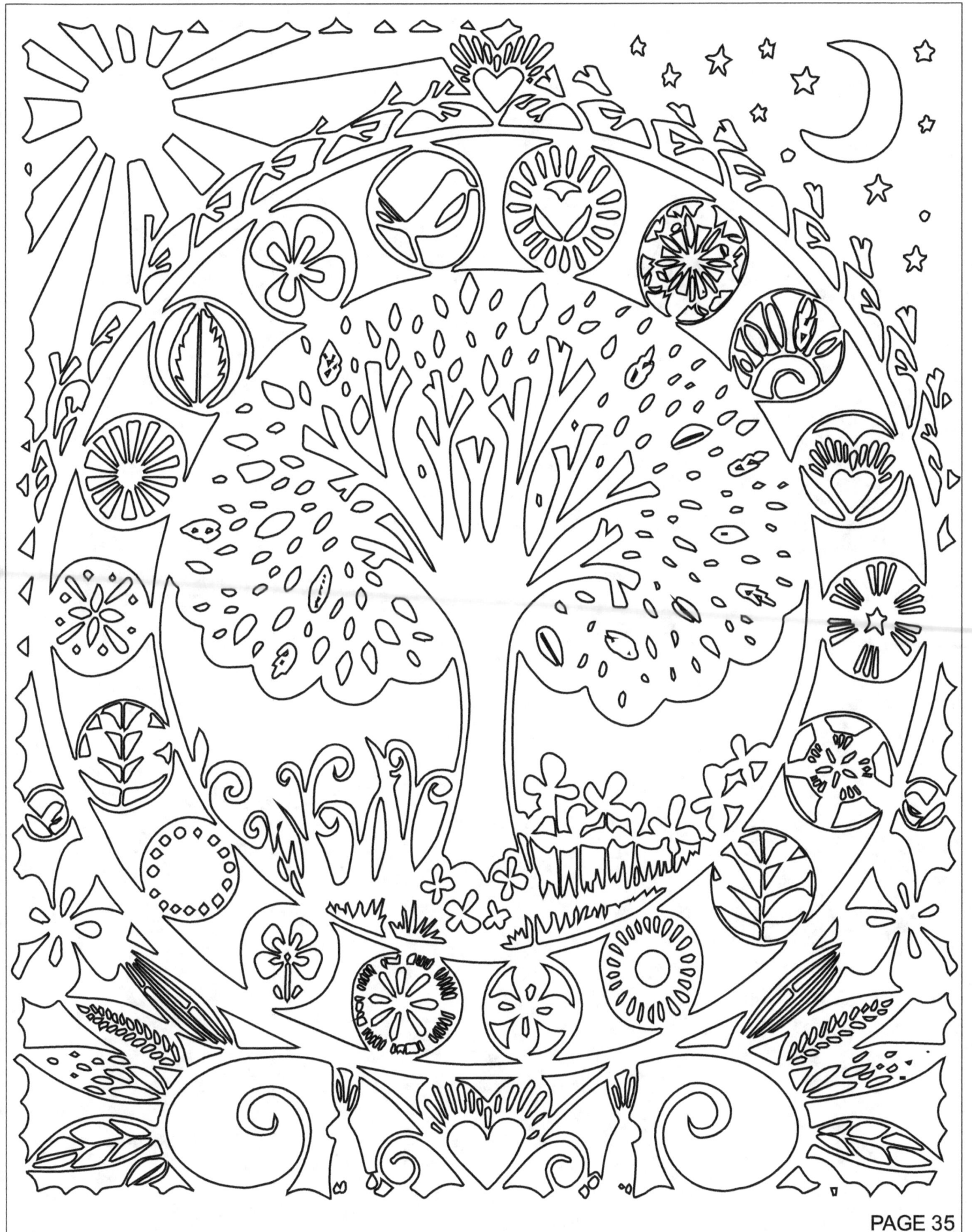

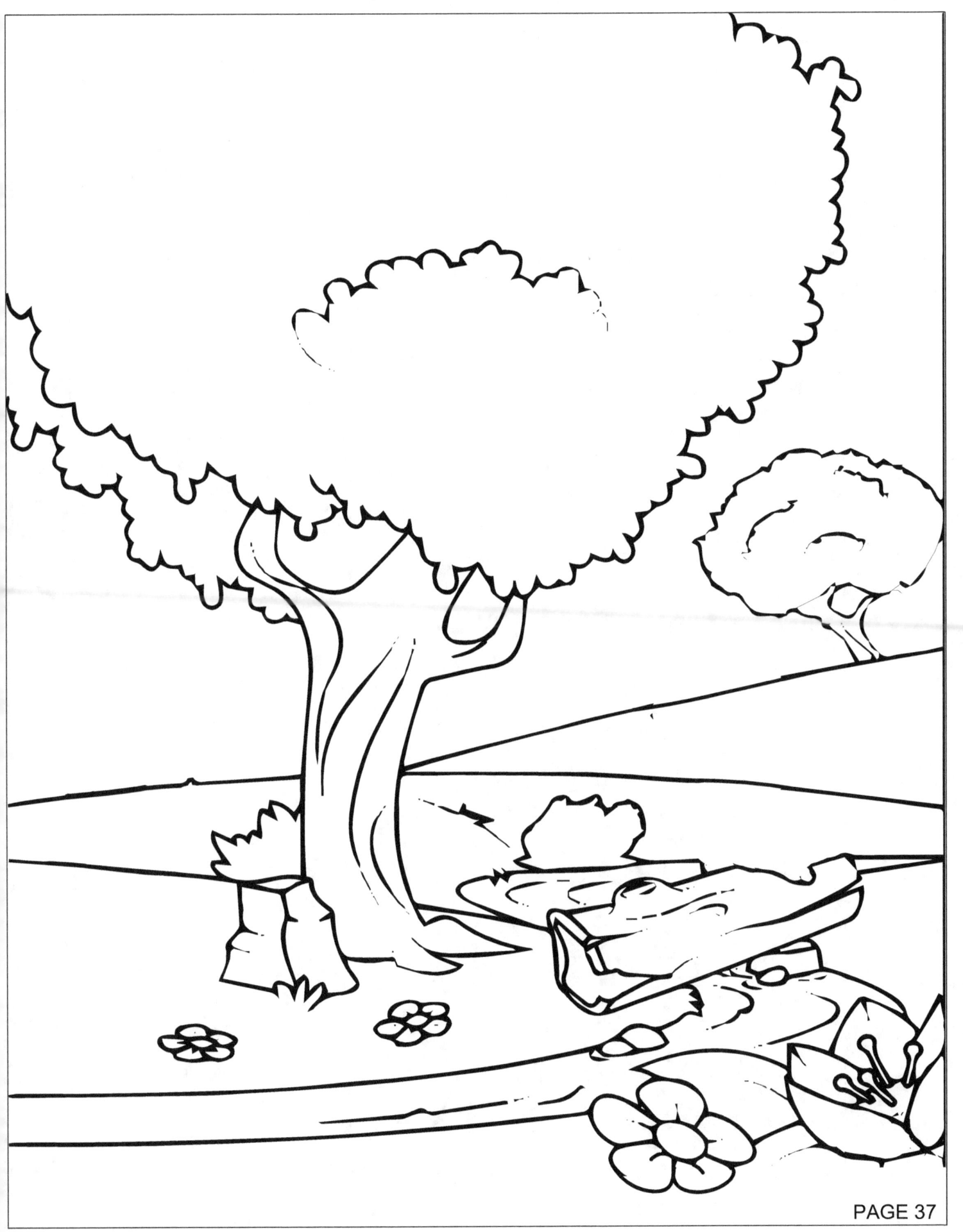

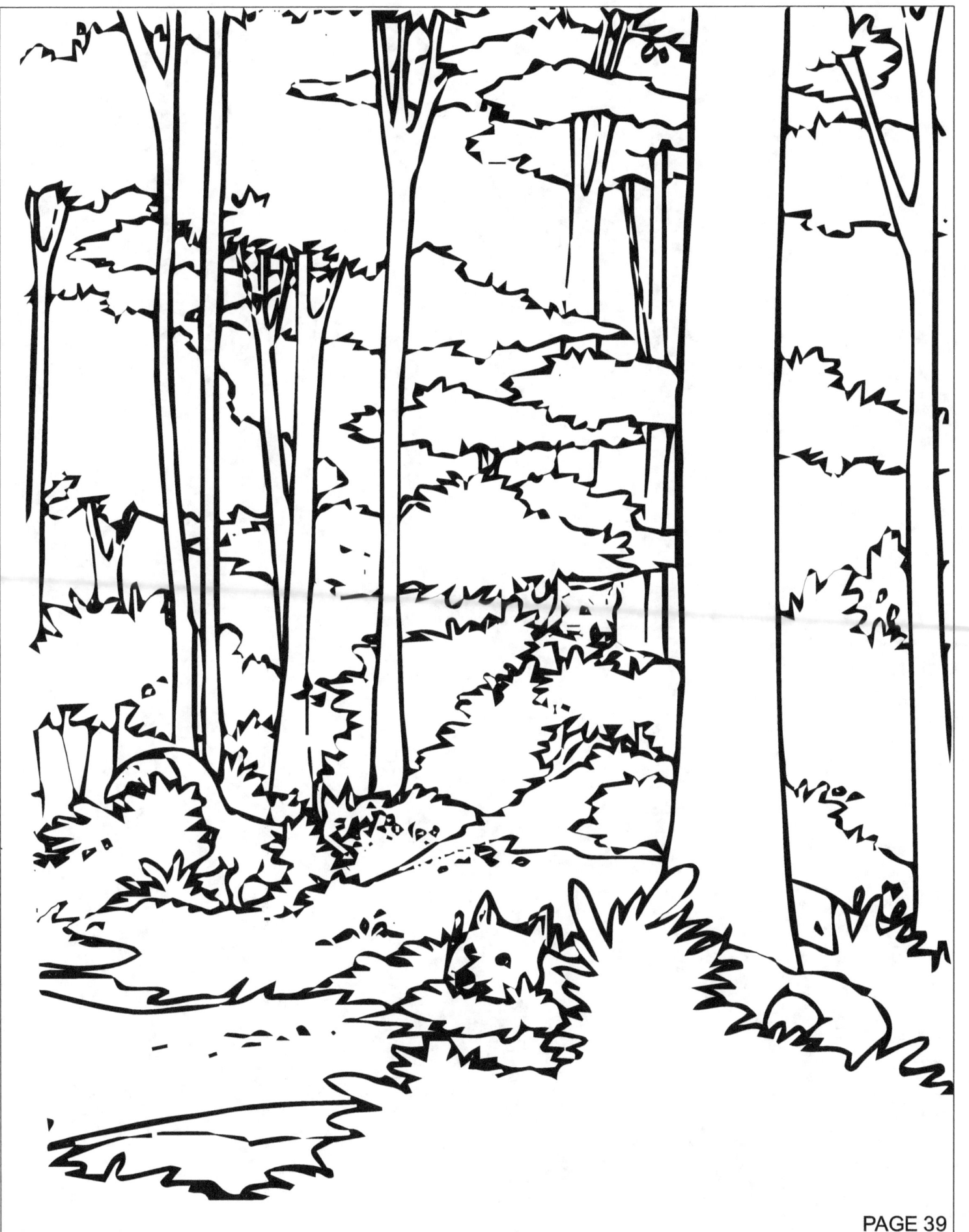

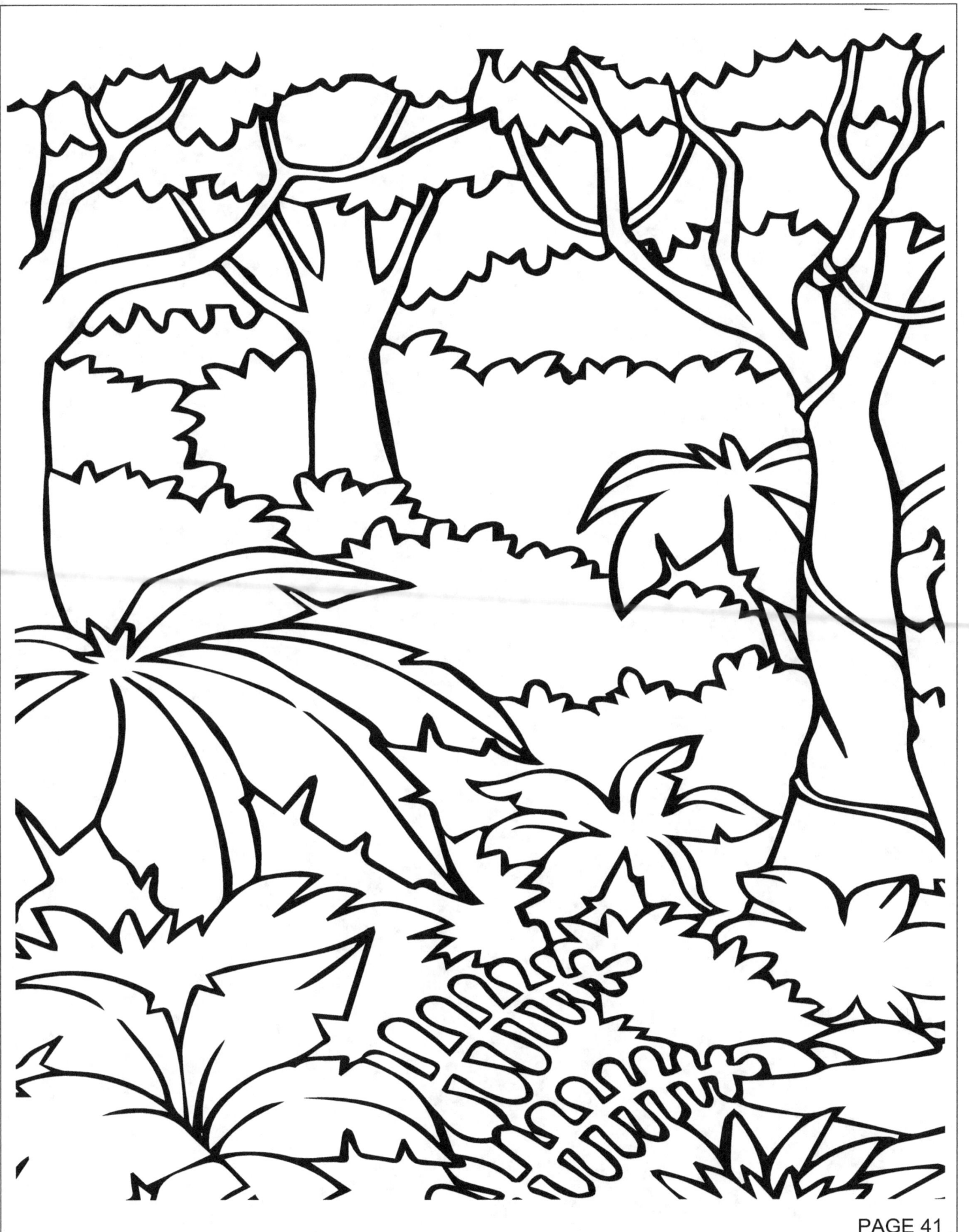

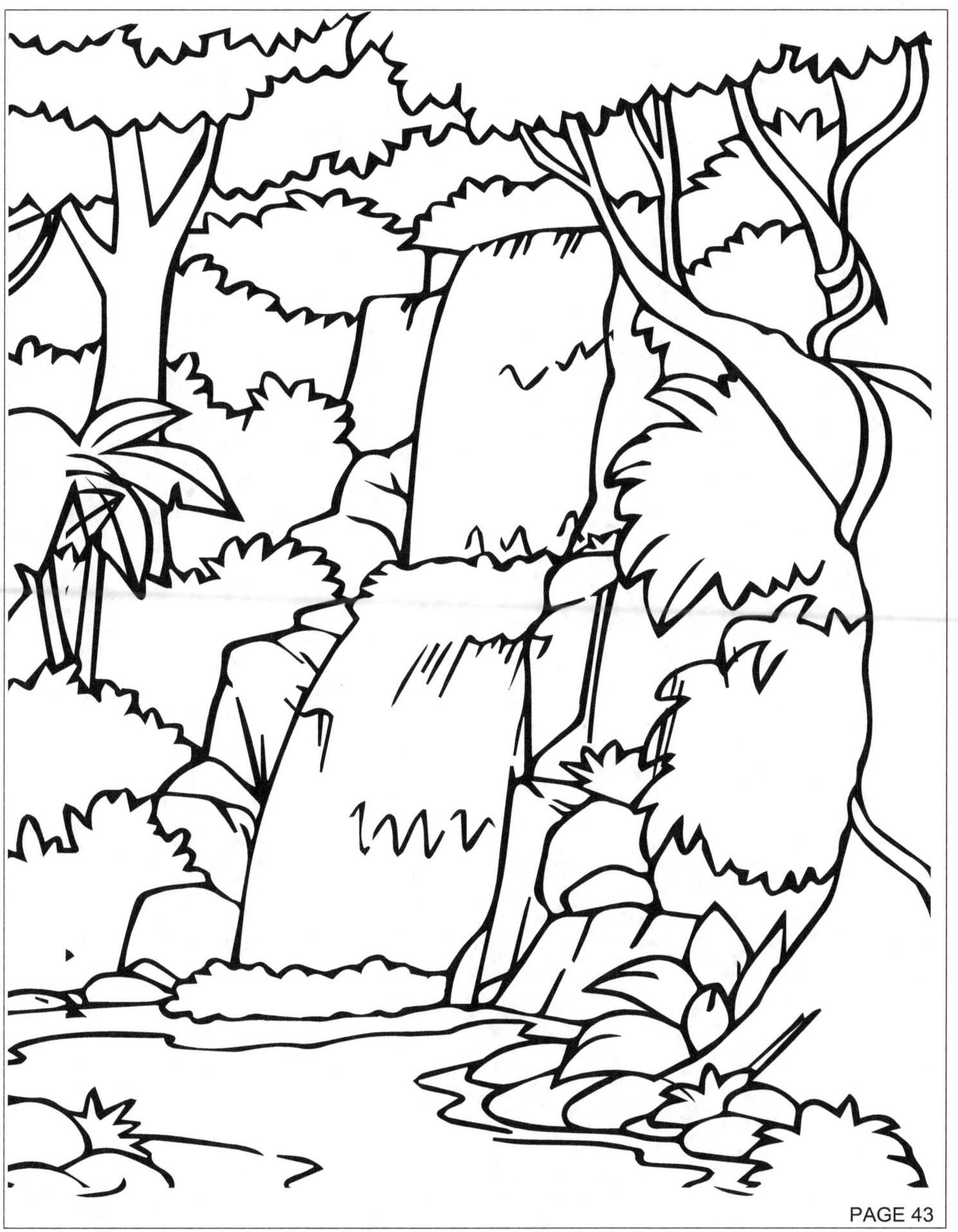

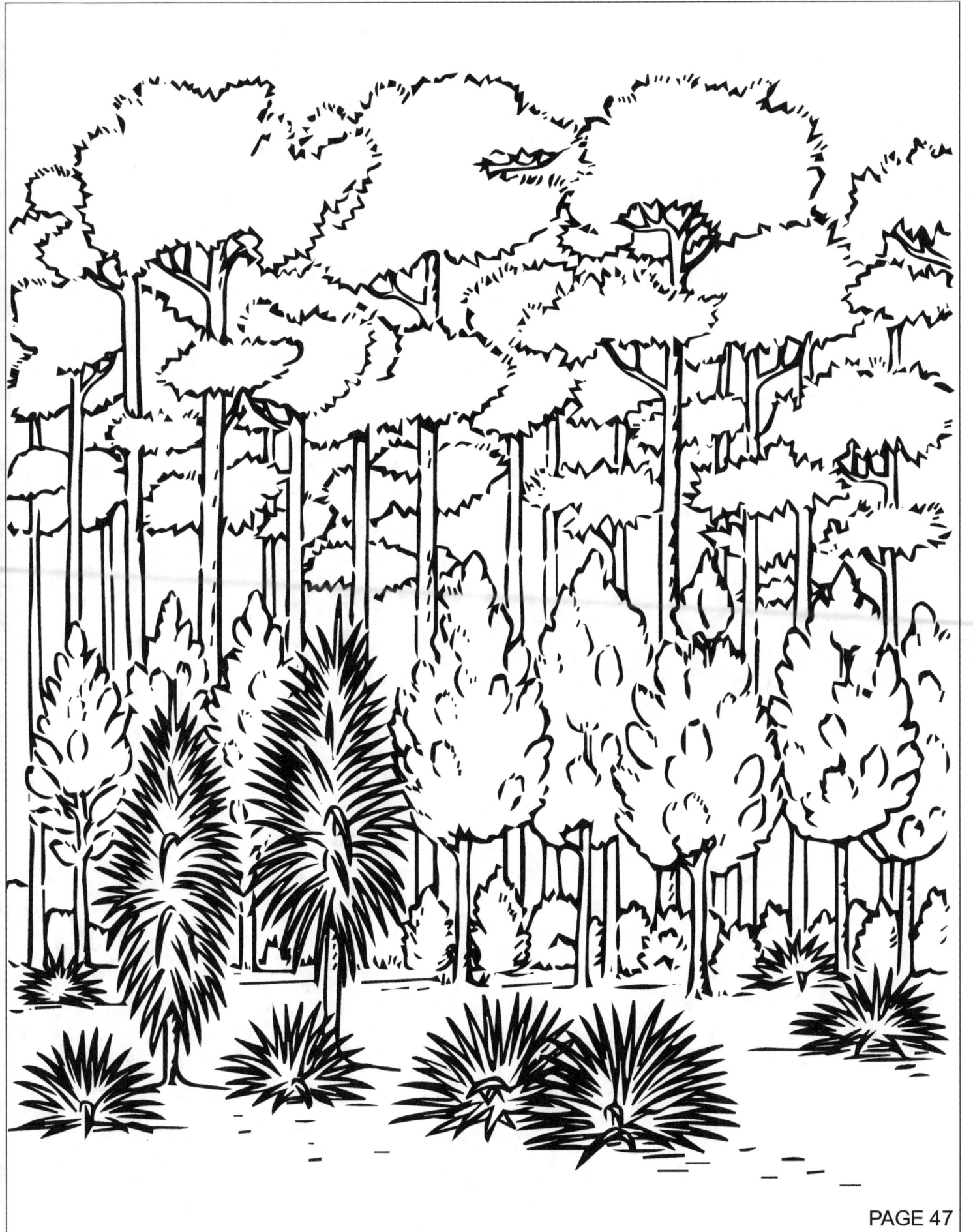

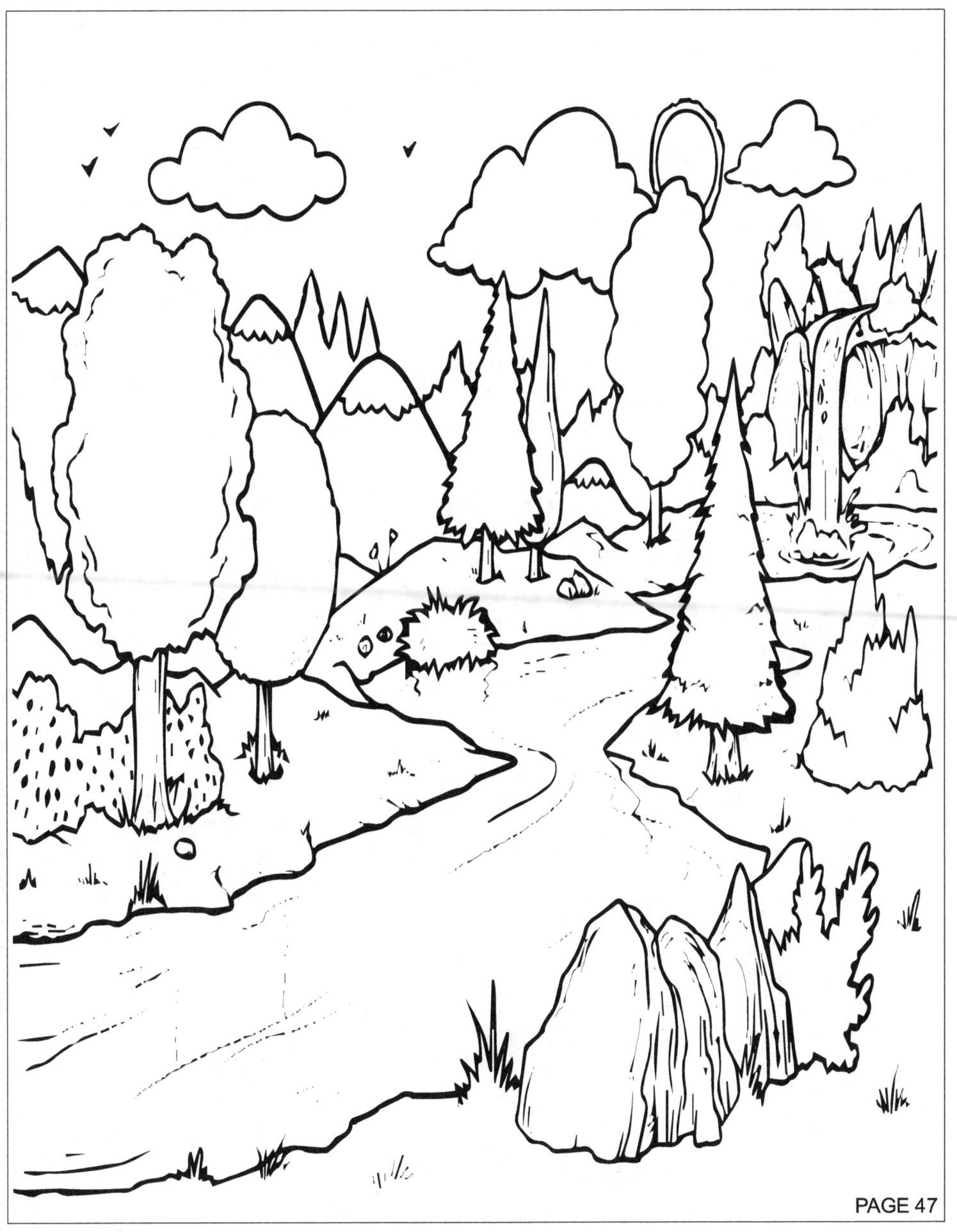

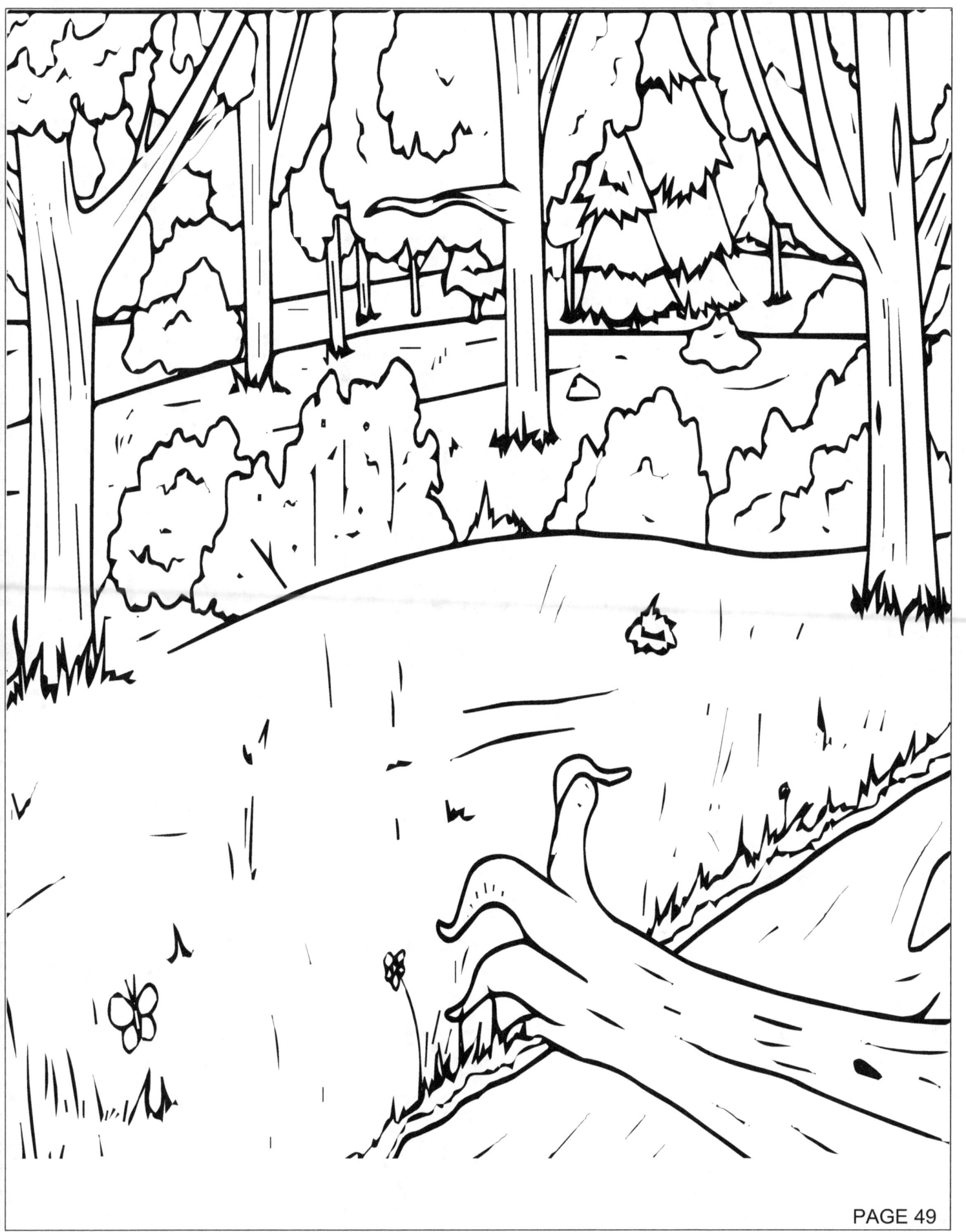

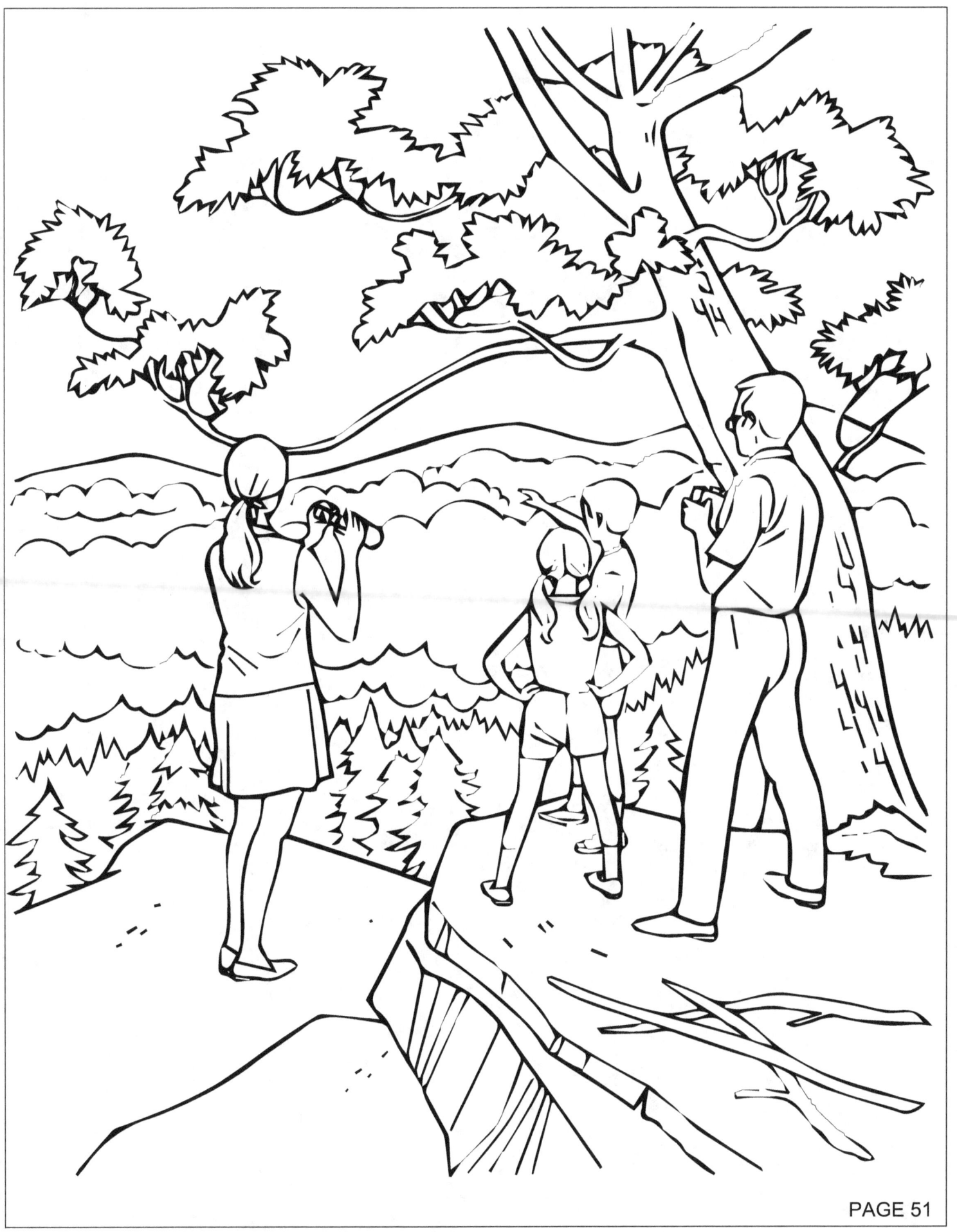

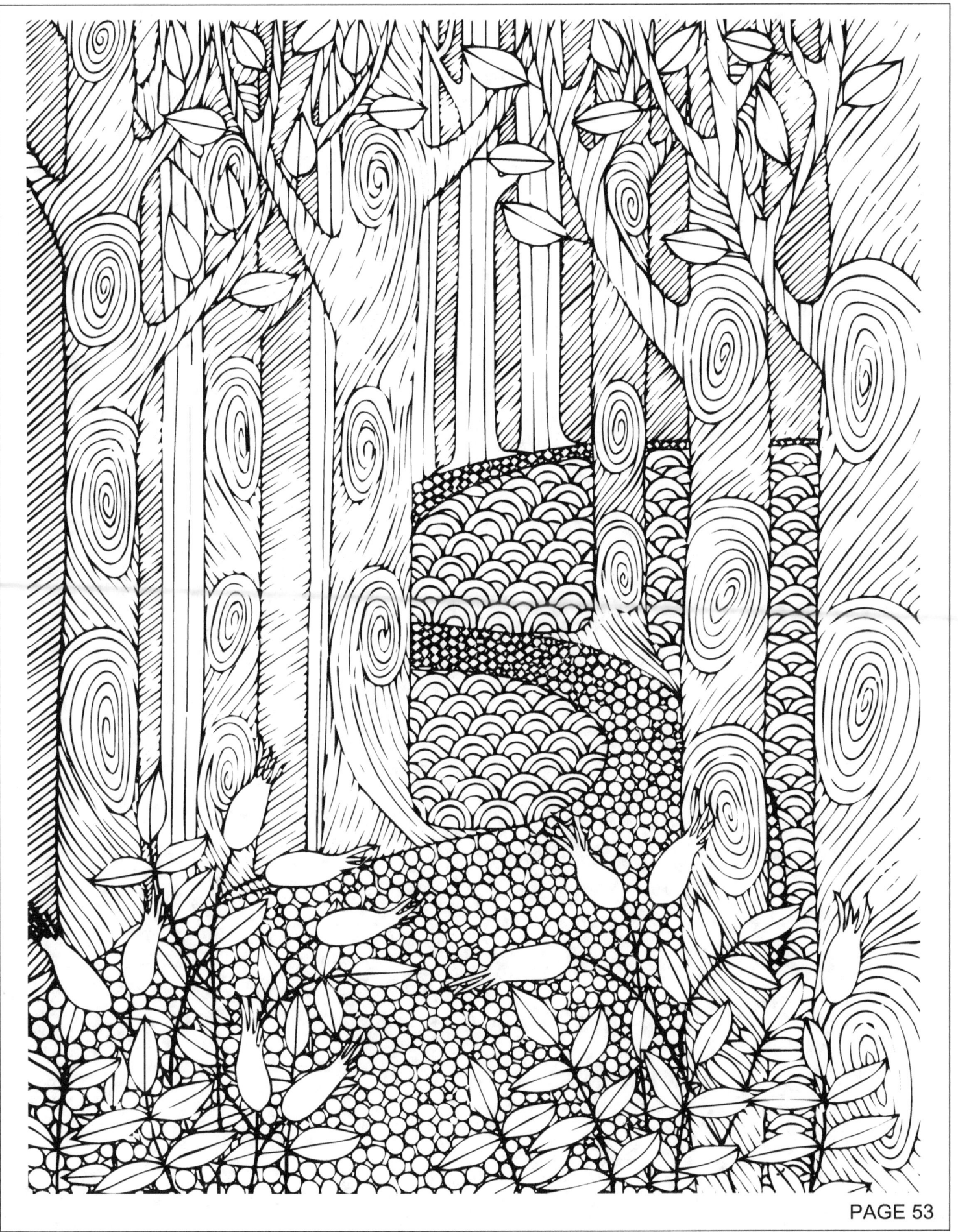

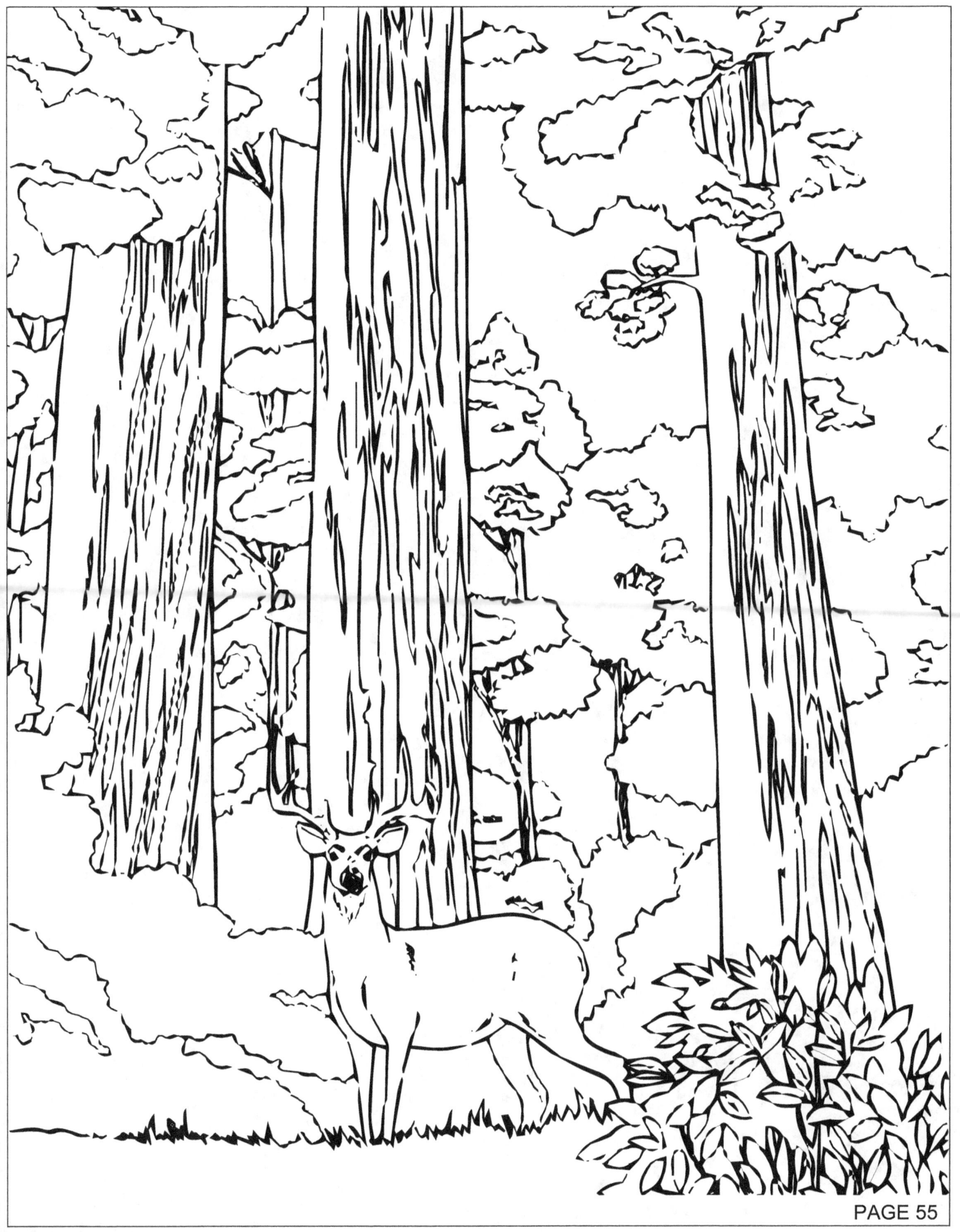

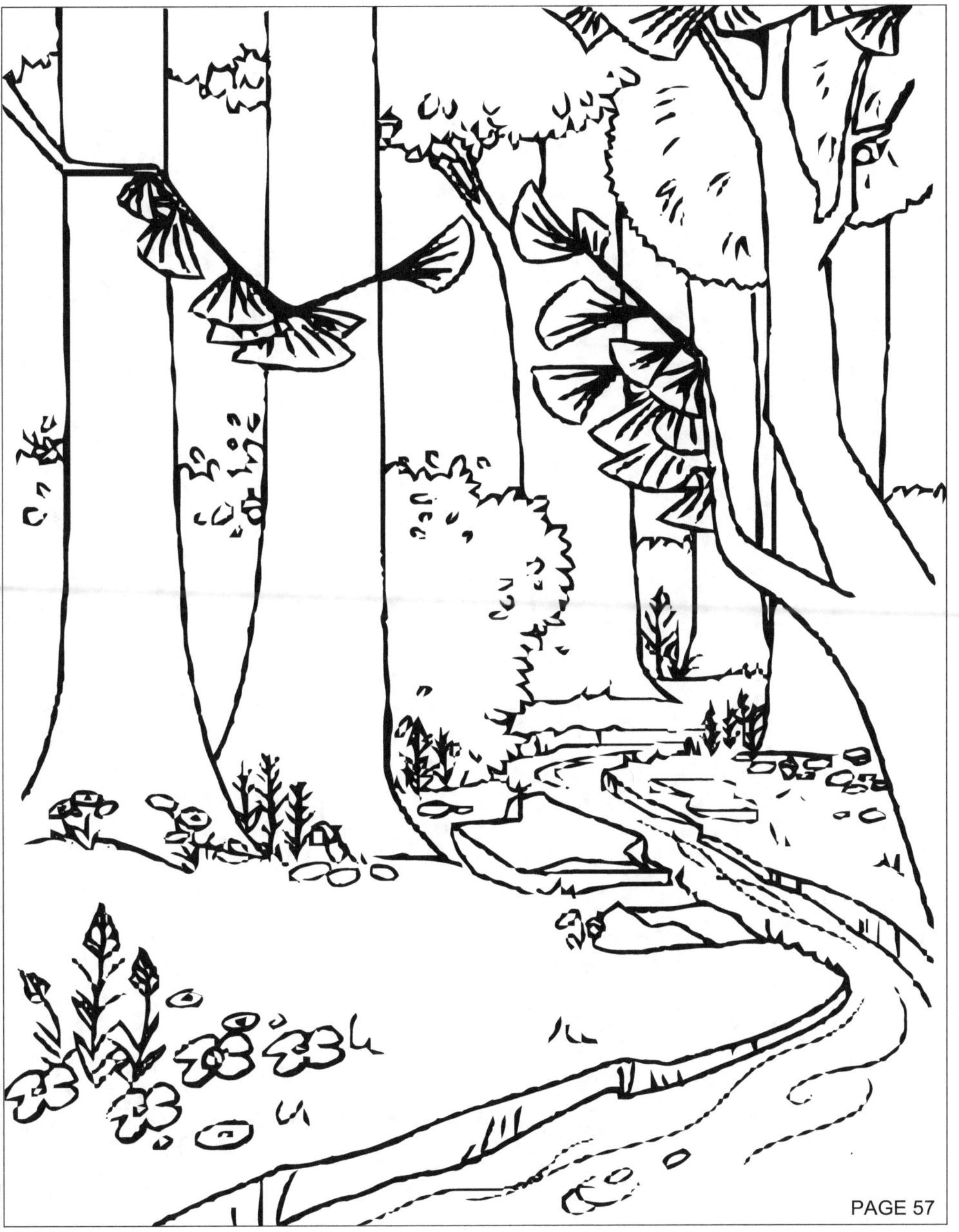

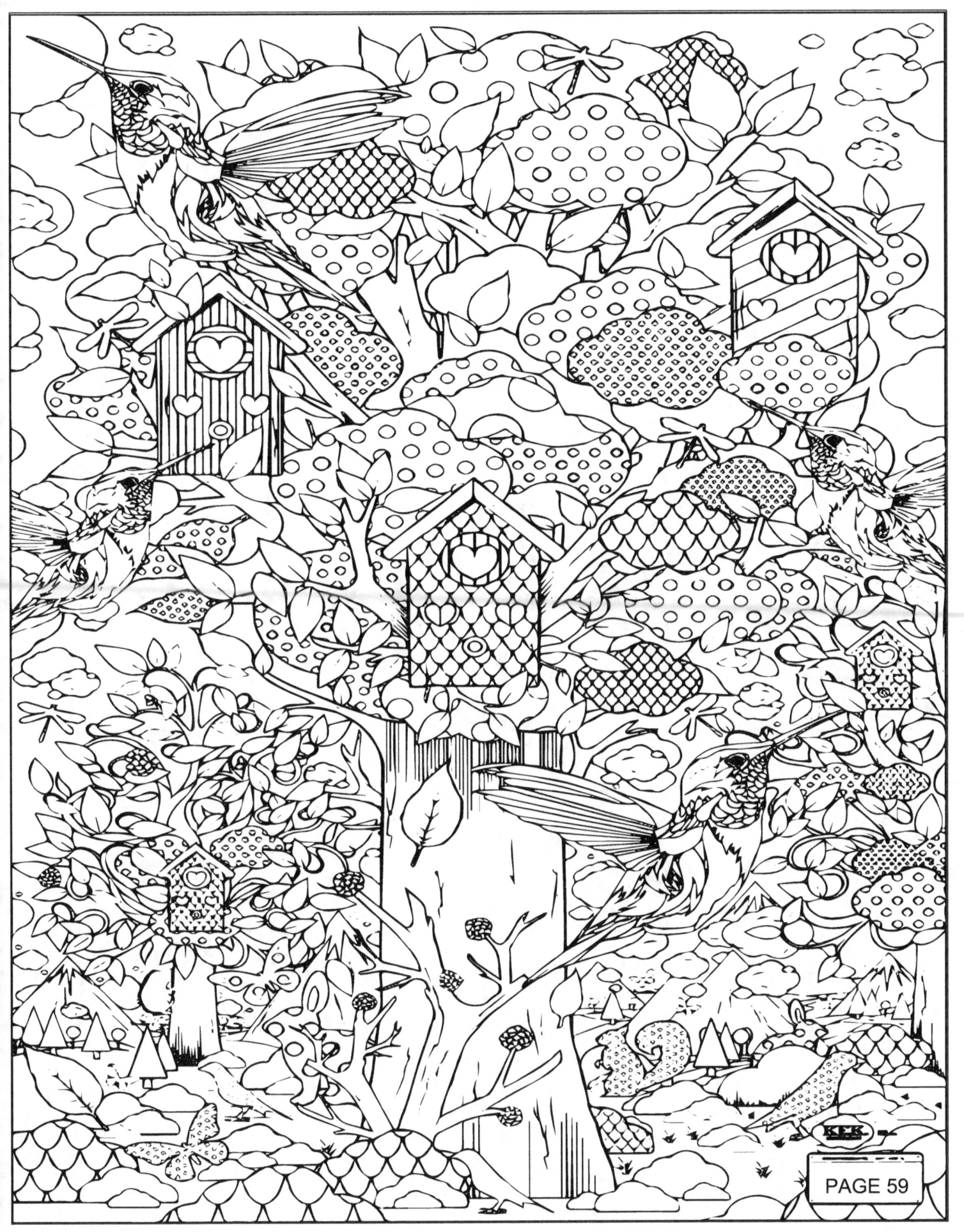

PAGE 59

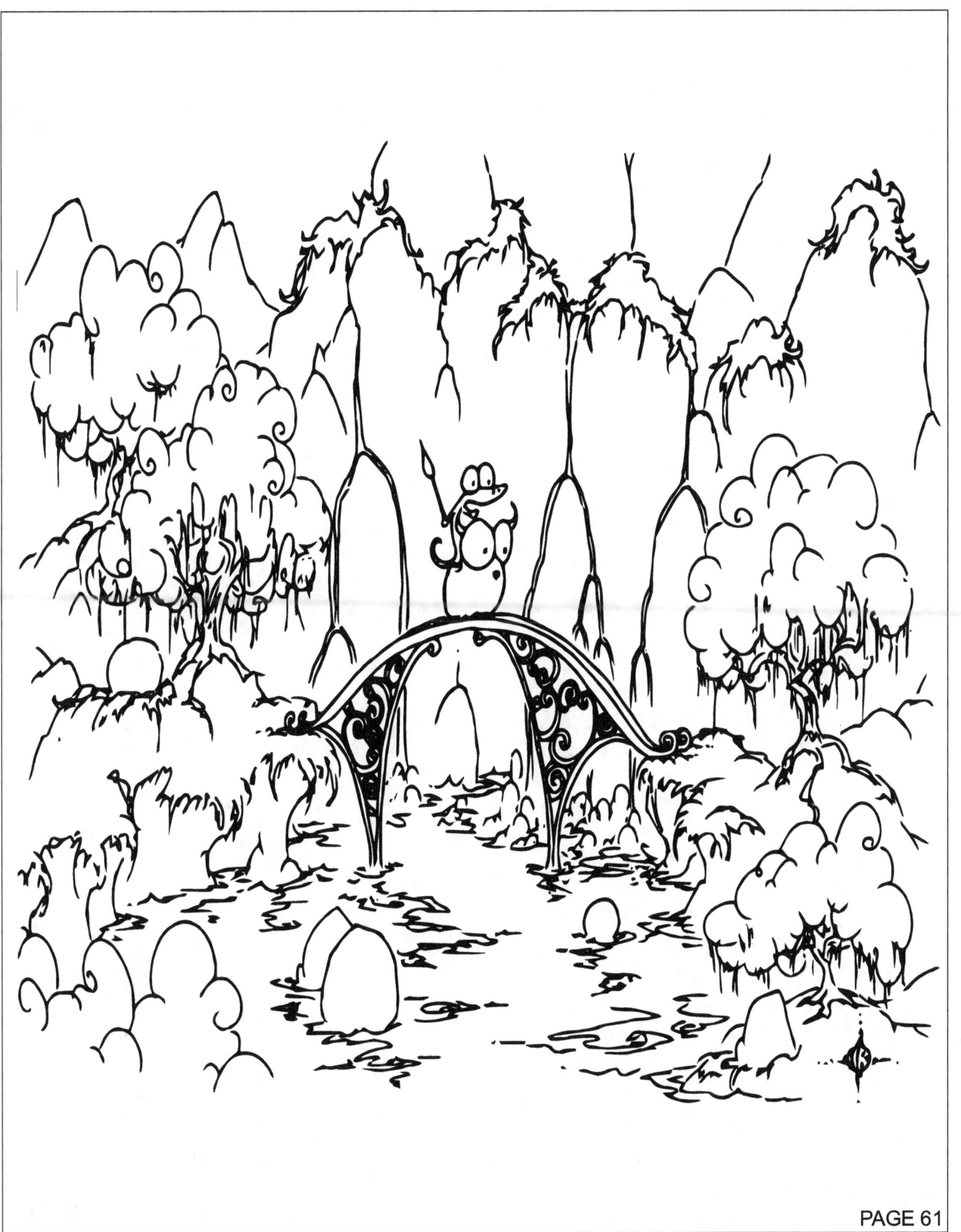

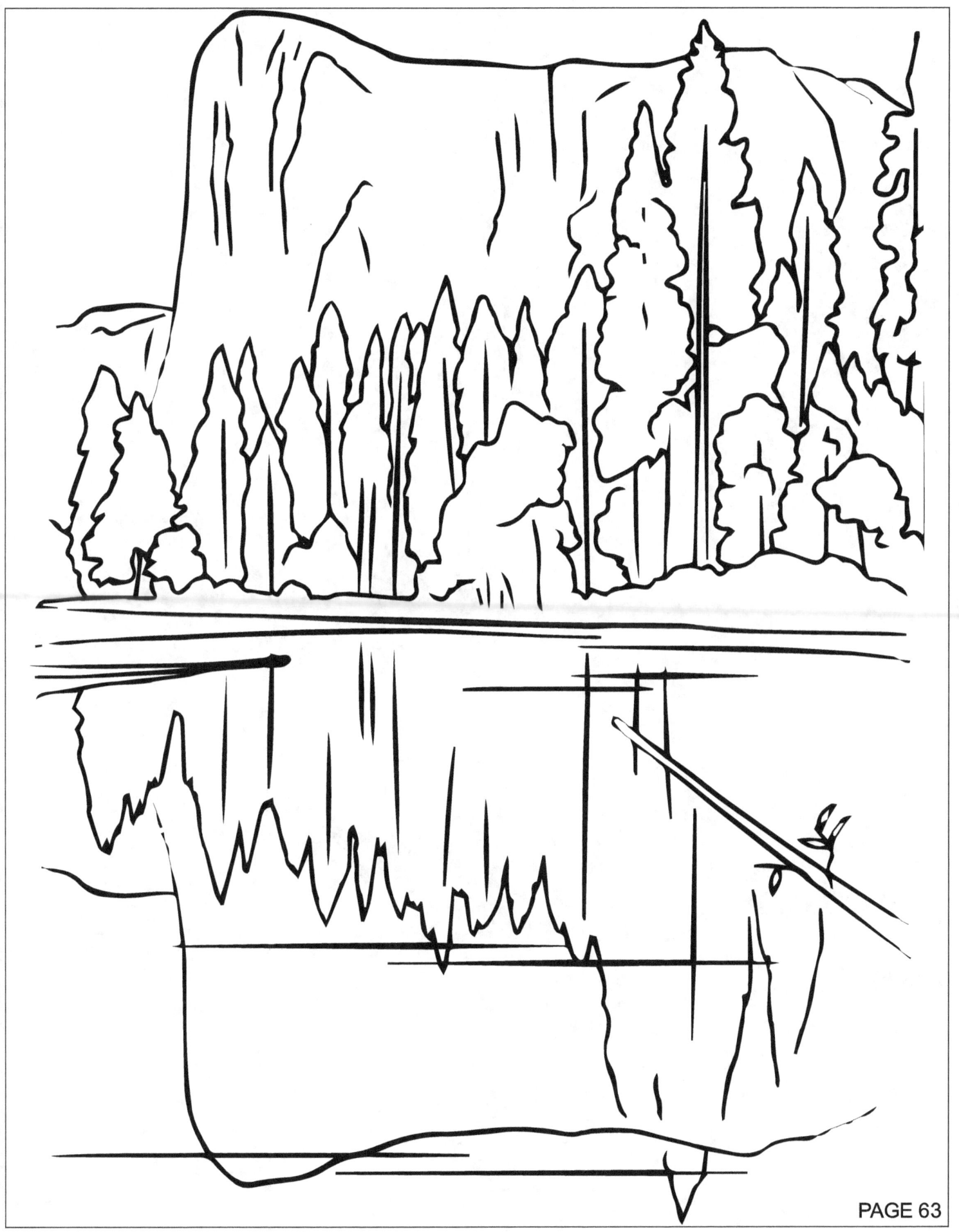

www.ingramcontent.com/pod-product-compliance
Lightning Source LLC
Chambersburg PA
CBHW081537220526
45467CB00010B/3232